Regency Square

Its history and its stories

Gill Wales &
Suzanne Hinton

First published in 2018 by Belle Vue Books on behalf of the Regency Square Area Society
www.regencybrighton.com

ISBN 978-0-9956032-1-9

Designed and typeset by Carnegie Book Production

Printed and bound in the UK by Cambrian Printers

Cover illustration: *View of Regency Square, Brighton (Engraving by Newman & Co.).*
Courtesy of Royal Pavilion & Museums, Brighton & Hove

Thanks and acknowledgements

This book would not have been possible without the treasure trove of original documents and other records at The Keep. Special thanks are due to the staff at The Keep, whose expertise and enthusiasm helped us uncover so much important information. We are also grateful for the resources available through the Regency Society of Brighton and Hove, the Royal Pavilion & Museums at Brighton & Hove, MyHouseMyStreet, and the special collections held by the Universities of Leicester and Nottingham.

No work of historical research stands in isolation. We are indebted to all the local historians in Sussex, London and South Wales whose work over many decades has provided such a solid base for this book. In particular, to Mr Chris Horlock for permission to use photographs and generously sharing other materials from his collection; to Mr Phil Jenkins of Industrial Wales for helping to ensure that the history of the early coalfields is not lost; to Mr David Robson MA RIBA for his invaluable expertise in architectural history.

Finally, we thank Mr Kevin Bacon, Digital Manager at the Royal Pavilion & Museums, Brighton & Hove, and Mr Tracy Wadey for their kind help in preparing images.

Every reasonable effort has been made to trace and acknowledge copyright of images. If any has been used without due acknowledgement, please contact the publisher so that a suitable amendment can be made on the Regency Square Area Society website and in any future edition.

Contents

Where and what is Regency Square?   **1**

Brighton before Regency Square   **2**

The old town   2

The land around the old town   3

Sea water cures   5

A fashionable resort   6

A military town   7

Brighton begins to grow   8

**The men behind Regency Square: Francis
and Joshua Flesher Hanson**   **11**

Francis Hanson   11

Belle Vue   12

Moving the West Mill   14

The Toy Fair   15

Fortunes decline   15

Joshua Flesher Hanson   16

The birth of Regency Square   **19**

Buying the land   19

An earlier development plan   20

The first house   20

The source of the money   23

The naming of Regency Square   23

Building begins   **26**

Who were the builders?   27

Variations in the building agreements   28

Building materials   28

Building workers   33

The rapid rise of Regency Square   **34**

   A significant landmark   36

   Progress slows   36

Design and architects   **39**

   The ground plan   39

   Overall design   40

   Who was the architect?   42

   The seafront corners   47

   No. 1: St Albans House   48

   Abbotts   52

   The north-east corner   55

   Regency Colonnade   61

Rates   **63**

Hanson's management of the development   **64**

   Roads   65

   John Vallance   65

   Enforcing the covenants   66

Inside the houses   **69**

   Kitchens and sculleries   70

   Water   70

   Heat, light and other comforts   71

No. 5: Canoodling in the parlour   **73**

Sewers and cess pits   **76**

The central gardens   **78**

   An exclusive space   78

   A car park   78

No. 18: From disaster to success   **82**

The mews   **84**

   Regency Mews   84

   Queensbury Mews   85

No. 45: Shots and screams   **89**

The seafront   **91**
   The Royal Sussex Regiment Memorial   92
   The West Pier   94

No. 21: A house of many talents   **95**

Regency Square's management committees   **101**
   1818–1884   101
   1885–1944   103
   Maintaining the lawn   104
   Complaints   106
   Regency Square Area Society, 1979–2018   108

A peep into other houses   **110**

What Hanson did next   **119**

Sources   **126**

Notes   **128**

Map: Regency Square neighbourhood   **129**

Subscribers   **131**

Index   **132**

My Dear Sister,

I'm in Brighton! How lucky I was to get this work. Lady's maid at last. And how tall this house is! You have no idea. When the carter stopped in front of it, I just looked up and up and up at it. But, my dear, when I climbed down from the cart, there was a brick pavement in front of the house not at all like the cobbles at home. I have a tiny room all to myself on the top floor. When I have a moment, I can just get a glimpse of the sea out of my little window. I don't know why this place is called a 'square'. There is nothing but a big empty space on the other side of the road – they call it a lawn – and it all seems rather deserted. Why do the master and mistress want to live here? Some of the houses in the row are not finished and they are certainly not ready to live in. This is such a strange, eerie place.

My love to all at home, your loving sister

Polly

Where and what is Regency Square?

Squares and crescents of tall, elegant houses around a central garden are a principal feature of Brighton and Hove's historic architecture. Regency Square was the first of the city's larger seafront squares, featuring a 1½ acre garden. It lies on Brighton's western seafront, midway between the old town and the boundary with Hove.

Arranging houses around a square or crescent increases the number of properties with a direct view of the sea. Regency Square is built on a slope, rising from 11 to 25 metres (36 to 82 feet) above sea level, maximising the sea view for all of the houses facing the garden.

Regency Square was begun in 1818, with most of its houses completed between 1820 and 1826. Almost all are still standing and would be outwardly recognisable to their builders. Internally, most have been converted into flats[1].

This book, produced to mark the bicentenary of Regency Square's beginnings, describes its origins, and its life and times.

---

1   At the time of writing, 10 hotels occupy 13 of the original houses. Two other houses have been converted into an office building. Regency Square is otherwise a mainly residential square: in 2013 it was home to 277 households.

Brighton before Regency Square

To understand how Brighton came to build so many grand squares and crescents, it's necessary to take a brief look at its history.

The parish of Brighton – or Brighthelmston as it was originally called – stretched from its border with Hove in the west, to Ovingdean in the east and Preston in the north[2]. Most of the parish was agricultural land until well into the 19th century. Until the late 18th century the town was contained within the area bounded by West Street, North Street and East Street – the area we now refer to as The Lanes. The parish church of St Nicholas stood above the town on Church Hill.

The old town

Brighthelmston was a market town and fishing port. In the early 16th century the town was almost completely burned to the ground during a raid by a French naval fleet. It recovered and prospered anew, becoming one of the largest towns in Sussex, with a population of 4,000 people, by the mid-17th century.

As well as the area we now call The Lanes there had been a lower town, inhabited by fishing families, on the foreshore below the cliff. The lower town was especially vulnerable to damage by storms: shops and houses were repeatedly flooded and swept away throughout the 1600s. Then, in 1703 and 1705, two enormous storms battered the entire country. Part of Brighthelmston's fishing fleet was lost at sea, the church and many houses in the upper town were damaged, the

---

2   The boundary between the parishes of Brighton and Preston followed the lines of the present day Old Shoreham and New England Roads as far as Ditchling Road, then along Hollingdean and Bear Roads. Brighton's boundary began to expand beyond these limits only at the end of the 19th century.

lower town destroyed completely. Baxter's Directory of 1822 states that these two storms destroyed 113 shops and cottages *under the cliff*, including the town's market house. It adds: *The walls of one of the streets that formerly stood under the Cliff were discovered in 1818 by some labourers. The ruins were buried under a layer of beach more than 15 feet thick.* The lower town of old Brighthelmston has remained beneath the seafront ever since.[3]

Brighthelmston was also a coastal trading port, receiving coal and other goods from London and the north of England, shipping out local produce in return. The lack of a harbour meant that its role as a trading port declined during the 18th century, just at the time that fishing also came under pressure.

This mix of misfortune and disadvantage meant that by the middle of the 18th century the population had plummeted to around 2,000 people.

The land around the old town

The agricultural land around the town was divided into field systems. The five field systems nearest the old town were called laines: Little Laine, immediately east of The Steyne (Old Steine today), is now the St James's Street area; the East Laine is now Kemp Town; Hilly Laine is the Hanover area; the North Laine lives on as the area between North Street and Trafalgar Street.

Each laine was divided into *furlongs*.[4] Regency Square would be built on two furlongs in the West Laine: the Cliff Butts and the Furlong Heading the Cliff Butts.

The farmland around the town was dotted with windmills. At any one point in the latter half of the 18th century there were at least half a dozen windmills within the parish. One of these, the West Mill, stood at the western end of the West Laine Cliff Butts between 1744 and 1797.

---

3   The natural foreshore at Brighton is solid chalk. After the storms of 1703 and 1705, wooden groynes were built on the foreshore near the town. Concrete groynes were built from 1867. Groynes cause shingle to accumulate, protecting the cliffs from erosion by the sea. Other sea defences were added in the 19th century, including sea walls along the cliff faces. Natural chalk foreshore can still be seen at low tide, east of the Marina at Black Rock.

4   Not to be confused with furlongs that are units of length.

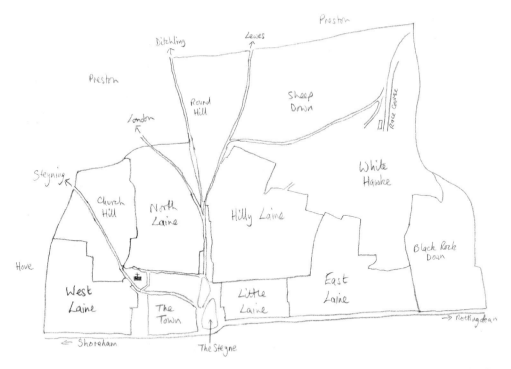

The field systems surrounding the old town of Brighton. Based on A Plan of the Parish of Brighthelmston 1792, AMS 4106 held by East Sussex Record Office at The Keep.

Furlongs were divided into narrow strips called *pauls* or *paulpieces*. A single paulpiece was roughly an eighth of an acre.[5] The legacy of the paulpieces can be seen in the Hanover, North Laine and St James's Street areas, where the narrow streets were constructed along paulpieces.

In some furlongs, all the paulpieces were owned by just one or two landlords; in others, ownership was split between several landowners. In 1792, the West Laine Furlong Heading the Cliff Butts contained 80 paulpieces, split between two landowners: the Duke of Dorset and Thomas Kemp. The neighbouring Cliff Butts furlong contained 101 paulpieces, divided between 12 different owners.

---

5   In the 18th century, the size of an acre was subject to local variation. It was not the same as a modern, standard acre.

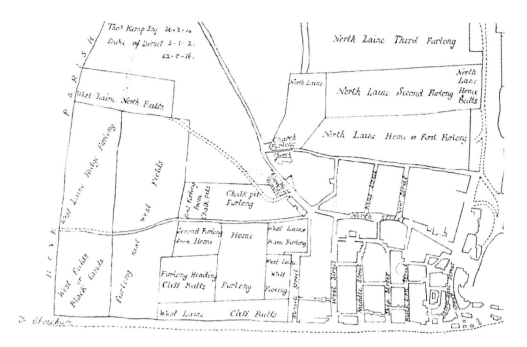

Extract of A Plan of the Parish of Brighthelmston 1792 showing the furlongs in the West Laine. Tracks known as leakways ran along the boundaries between furlongs. Many of the major roads within central Brighton follow the lines of these ancient leakways. The track running between the West Laine's Chalk Pit and Home furlongs became Western Road. AMS 4106 Courtesy of East Sussex Record Office at The Keep.

Sea water cures

In 1750, a Lewes physician called Dr Richard Russell published a paper advocating sea water – drinking it as well as bathing in it – as a remedy for various maladies. Mineral spring and spa waters had been regarded as healthful for centuries, but sea water as a 'cure' was relatively new. A physician in Scarborough is credited with being the first to promote the idea.

Dr Russell's advice struck a chord among the upper and middle classes, who started to come to Brighton to be cured of their ills. In some cases, they *were* cured, or at least made to feel healthier, because much of his advice can be summed up as fresh air, exercise and hygiene – having a wash being a rare event for most people in the 18th century. The mere act of bathing in sea water, whose salt content makes it slightly antiseptic, helped some skin complaints. Drinking sea water may have helped purge the consequences of over-eating and the iodine content may have helped people with goitre (swollen thyroid glands).

Brighton's proximity to the county town of Lewes probably made it the obvious place for Dr Russell to provide patients with a sea water cure. The chalybeate spring at St Ann's Well in Hove meant that both the new and traditional types of 'taking the waters' could be prescribed.

Other physicians began to offer the sea water cure at Brighton. Dr John Awsiter built a sea water bath house, pumping the sea indoors and warming it up for those too timid to brave the waves. Other indoor bathing establishments followed.

Visitors seeking sea water cures needed places to stay, meals and entertainments. The local population was happy to oblige. Bathing machines and pleasure boats were introduced, libraries, coffee houses and assembly rooms began to appear, the number of inns and lodging houses increased. Brighton was re-invented as a health resort.

A fashionable resort

At first, the number of visitors to the town could be measured in the hundreds, but by the latter years of the 18th century they are believed to have been arriving in their thousands, outnumbering the locals.

A coincidental development at this time helped Brighton's emergence as a resort. In spite of being relatively near to London, haphazard maintenance and the heavy clay of Sussex made the roads to Brighton difficult to negotiate in wet weather. In 1750, when Dr Russell published his paper on the health benefits of sea water, there was only one coach a week from London to Brighton and it took two days to complete the journey. Large loads of heavy goods were easier to transport by sea than by road.

During the course of the 18th century, Britain introduced turnpike trusts to maintain highways, partially funding the work through tolls. These began to have an impact in Sussex in the 1760s. The speed and frequency of coach services between London and Brighton, and between Brighton and other towns, increased. By 1788, there were five coaches from London every day during the summer, the journey taking eight hours.

Probably the biggest boost to the town's development as a fashionable resort was the arrival of the Prince of Wales, later to become the Prince Regent (1811) and eventually crowned King George IV (1820). The Prince of Wales' first trip to the town, in September 1783, was to visit his uncle, the Duke of Cumberland, who was renting a house on the Steyne. The prince liked the town and decided to rent a home here for himself, later building a villa (the Marine Pavilion), eventually transforming it into a palace, the Royal Pavilion.

The adoption of Brighton by the heir to the throne confirmed the town as a place to see and be seen.

A military town

Britain was engaged in many overseas wars throughout the 18th century. From 1793 the country was at war with post-revolutionary France. Fearful of invasion from across the Channel, the government took defensive steps.

Military encampments began to take place along the south coast, including at Brighton. The first of the Brighton encampments, in 1793, involved 10,000 troops from 14 regiments. It lasted for 10 weeks, from mid-August to late October, and spread across the whole of the West Laine, from the edge of the town to the border with Hove.

Encampments at Brighton became an almost annual event between 1793 and 1803, although not always at the same sites. The 1794 encampment was based at the Race Hill, the 1798 encampment just over the border in Preston parish. The purpose of the encampments was military training, but they also became a significant part of the social season, the exercises and mock battles providing spectacle for visitors. As described in Jane Austen's *Pride and Prejudice*, the presence of so many dashing young officers held a certain appeal for young, single women.[6]

---

6   *In Lydia's imagination, a visit to Brighton comprised every possibility of earthly happiness. She saw… the streets of that gay bathing-place covered with officers. She saw…..all the glories of the camp, its tents stretched forth in beauteous uniformity of lines, crowded with the young and gay, and dazzling with scarlet. To complete the view, she saw herself seated beneath a tent, tenderly flirting with at least six officers at once.* Pride and Prejudice, Jane Austen (1813)

Brighton begins to grow

In 1770 the town of Brighton had consisted of only seven principal streets, containing fewer than 600 houses, occupied by little more than 3,000 people. Thirty years later, the town had 18 streets, 1,500 houses and a population of just over 7,000.

Brighton was not the only town to see its population grow in the late 18th century. All over the country, people were moving from rural areas to towns and cities in search of work. Brighton's development as a resort meant that it was creating jobs in providing for visitors' needs.

In 1800, almost a third of the town's 1,500 houses provided visitor accommodation: there were 212 lodging houses (for the wealthiest visitors, who rented a whole house for their entourage), seven boarding houses and a further 208 establishments providing rooms to let. As well as accommodation, visitors created demand for shops and other services, including stabling for the many horses that transported people and goods to and around the town. The people working in these service industries also needed places to live.

The built-up area of Brighton began to expand beyond the old town. The new developments included grand houses in prime positions for the social elite and large furnished houses for the wealthy middle classes; shops and other commercial services; and streets of small houses and tenements for workers and their families.

The initial expansion was mainly to the east and north of the old town: Marlborough Place, Pavilion Parade, Old Steine; St James's Street, New Steine and the Marine Parade; plus narrow streets of shops and tradesmen behind North Street and St James's Street. To the west, new development was initially limited to the area between West Street and Artillery Place (now the site of the Grand Hotel).

In the 30 years between 1770 and 1800, the population of Brighton had more than doubled. By 1811, it had almost doubled again: the resident population was now 12,000 people and the number of houses nudging 2,500. The construction of grand houses had continued to spread along the London and Lewes roads, at Gloucester Place, Grand Parade, Richmond Place and

York Place. Development had also continued to the east and north. On Hilly Laine, narrow streets for the working classes were built, creating the Albion Hill, Carlton Hill and Edward Street areas.

To the west of the town, construction of Bedford and Russell squares, Cannon Place and Grenville Place had begun; and increasing numbers of villas were built along the western seafront. It's shortly after this point that Regency Square enters the picture.

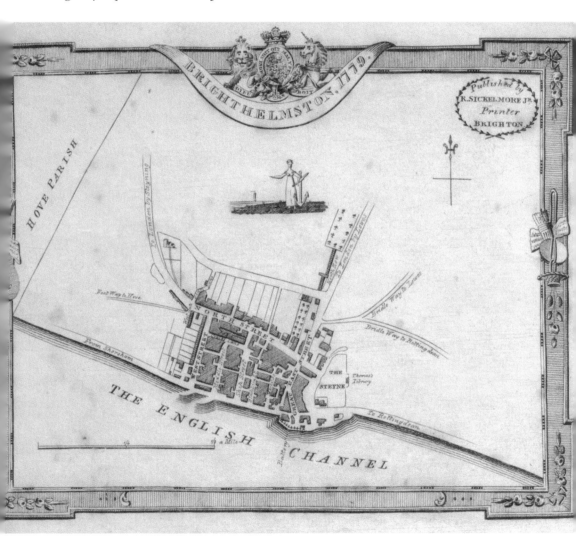

Map of Brighthelmston 1779, by R. Sicklemore Junior.
Courtesy of Royal Pavilion & Museums, Brighton & Hove

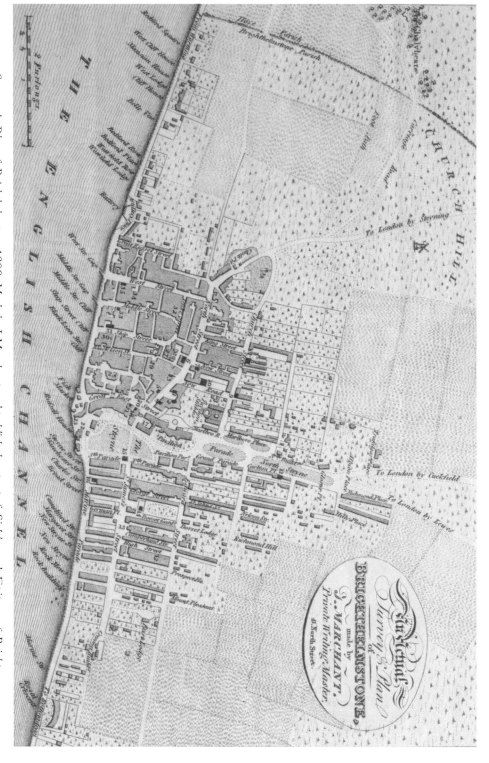

Survey & Plan of Brighthelmstone 1809. Made by J Marchant and published as part of Sicklemore's Epitome of Brighton. Courtesy of Royal Pavilion & Museums, Brighton & Hove

The men behind Regency Square: Francis and Joshua Flesher Hanson

The man who is generally said to have created Regency Square is Joshua Flesher Hanson. He was a Londoner, born in 1782 in the parish of St Clement Danes, the eldest son of Francis and Martha Hanson. His unusual middle name honours his maternal grandmother, whose maiden name was Flesher.

But the story of Regency Square really begins with Joshua's father, Francis Hanson.

Francis Hanson

Francis Hanson was a textiles merchant, born in the City of London in 1756. He had a home and premises in Drury Lane at the time of Joshua's birth, and offices in the City of London in the 1790s.

Francis' father and grandfather – both named Samuel – had been orange merchants in the City. They imported oranges and other fruits from various Mediterranean countries, later adding sugar and rum to the goods they carried. At least one of Francis' brothers entered the family business, but Francis followed a different career path as a Blackwell Hall factor.

Blackwell Hall, in the City of London, was the centre of England's textiles trade. Factors supplied manufacturers with wool, held stocks of woven cloth in their London warehouses, and negotiated sales of the cloth to wholesalers, tailors and retailers. They advised manufacturers on changing fashions and the types of cloth that were likely to be in demand, and checked that all cloth passing through their warehouses was free of defects. Crucially, they also provided credit to manufacturers and buyers, which meant maintaining close links to City financiers.

The latter part of the 18th century was a boom time for the textiles industry, thanks to the combined effects of the Industrial Revolution, Britain's expanding colonial interests and her near-constant involvement in wars in Europe, as well as in the American Revolutionary War. The technological advances of the Industrial Revolution meant that cloth could be produced more quickly and cheaply than ever before. Britain's growing dominance in international trade provided access to both raw materials and potential markets; while the wars generated a huge market for cloth, as uniforms for the military.

Francis Hanson mainly traded in high quality cloth from traditional manufacturers in the West Country. The market for quality cloth was also thriving, thanks to the newly emerging middle class: people with disposable income wanting high status goods, including clothes and furnishings.

Francis apprenticed his eldest son, Joshua Flesher Hanson, to the Worshipful Company of Clothworkers in 1796. By this time, apprenticeship to a Livery Company was not necessarily with the intention of working at a particular trade. It was also the only route to becoming a freeman of the City of London. This was important, as only a freeman could ply any kind of trade in the City.

Belle Vue

In 1793, Francis Hanson started buying land in the West Laine of Brighton. His first purchase was a 29ft-wide plot at the western end of the Cliff Butts. He bought the plot for £100 and built a seafront villa, naming it Belle Vue House. It was one of a pair of villas, the other built and occupied by another Londoner, Charles Heath. Both villas were collectively known as Belle Vue.

Belle Vue House was not Francis Hanson's only home: during the 1790s, he also had a house in Islington. But Brighton became a significant part of his family life. The Brighton directories of 1799 and 1800 list Francis Hanson as one of the *principal inhabitants* of the town, giving his address as *Bellevue*. His youngest daughter, Martha, published a volume of poetry written at Belle Vue in the early 1800s and was married at St Nicholas' Church in 1825.

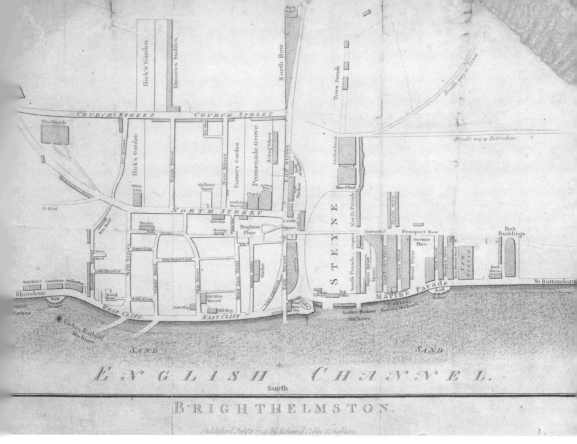

Map of Brighthelmston 1799. Published by Edward Cobby. Belle Vue is on the Road to Shoreham, extreme left.
Courtesy of Royal Pavilion & Museums, Brighton and Hove.

Belle Vue House became 132 Kings Road, currently the site of the Melrose Restaurant, between Regency Square and Preston Street.

Over a period of several years, Francis acquired another 13 acres[7] in the Cliff Butts and the Furlong Heading the Cliff Butts. He built a coach house and stables between what is now Preston Street and Little Preston Street. This spot was at the edge of a furlong, alongside an ancient track, possibly a more convenient place for a coach house and stables than the back of Belle Vue House.

As well as land, Francis acquired a wharf on the foreshore. The wharf stood below the cliff opposite what is now Regency Square's south-east corner. In his History of Brighthelmston, John Erredge described the wharf as *protected*

---

7   As measured by local custom, not today's standard acre.

by a strongly built brick wall, with shipways for repairing *moderately sized craft.* The hawser for hauling boats onto the shipways ran from the beach to a large capstan on the cliff, via a small tunnel under the cliff top road. The wharf is understood to have remained in operation until it was lost in one of the Kings Road improvement schemes.

Moving the West Mill

The Belle Vue villas were built next door to the West Mill, then owned by Mr John Streeter. In 1797 Mr Streeter was obliged to move the mill to a new location, allegedly because the new neighbours complained that it caused a nuisance. Francis Hanson was one of the neighbours, but he subsequently

This Mill was drawn from the spot now called Regency Square to Preston (a distance of two Miles), on the 28th March, 1797,

BY EIGHTY-SIX OXEN,

belonging to the following Gentlemen :—W. STANFORD, Esq., Messrs. HODSON, HAMSHAR, SCRASE, TRILL. HALL. and HARDWICKE. The Expedition was commanded by Mr. T. HODSON.

Moving the West Mill
James Gray Collection, Courtesy of the Regency Society

bought the plot on which the West Mill had stood, so it may in fact have been moved by mutual agreement.

Either way, moving the West Mill was a major undertaking. Various local farmers loaned 86 oxen to drag the mill two miles uphill to its new position in Dyke Road.

The Toy Fair

Brighthelmston's Toy Fair took place every year on 4 September. It was originally held on the cliff in front of Ship Street and Black Lion Street. Stalls, constructed from boat sails, spars and ropes, were run by fisherwomen, with roundabouts on the open space behind The Thatched House pub in Black Lion Street. In its heyday, the fair included travelling theatres and *freak shows*.

By the end of the 18th century, the fair was outgrowing its traditional location. It was moved to several new sites in the early 1800s, including to land north of The Level and finally to the Race Hill. One of its temporary homes was *Belle Vue Field*.[8]

Fortunes decline

Francis Hanson had been a successful business man. When his father died, in 1798, he bequeathed Francis only a token sum of £5 because he was already *amply provided for*. But in 1806 Francis was in serious financial difficulty and by 1808 his business had ceased trading.

His difficulties were partly linked to the focus of the textiles trade shifting to the North of England. Although his business had principally been concerned with West Country cloth, he had established trading links with the new northern manufacturers – indeed, his wife Martha was a Yorkshire woman. But the northern trade operated on a different basis from the traditional system, making it less profitable for factors.

---

8   Some sources state that Regency Square was built on *Belle Vue Field*. We have found no reference to the site being called Belle Vue before Francis Hanson and Charles Heath built their villas. Official documents continued to refer to the site by its furlong names. But it may have become informally known as Belle Vue Field when hosting the Toy Fair.

In addition, while Britain's wars with France increased demand for certain types of cloth, it depressed demand for the fine fabrics in which Francis Hanson specialised. He struggled to find a market for high quality cloth and the manufacturers to whom he had extended credit became slow to pay their debts.

Francis must have hoped that he could trade his way out of trouble by venturing into new markets. He began trading with the United States, but this only made matters worse, many of his American sales ending as bad debts.

Creditors took over Belle Vue House in 1812. In December 1813, Francis Hanson's remaining 13 acres in Brighton's West Laine were *assigned* (transferred) to a group of creditors led by his son-in-law, John Austin.

Joshua Flesher Hanson

When Francis Hanson's financial difficulties were coming to a head, his son Joshua Flesher Hanson was in charge of a private school in the City of London. The Little Tower Street Academy had been founded 100 years previously, specialising in mathematics and accountancy, subsequently offering a wide curriculum in science, technical and commercial subjects. Joshua Flesher Hanson was joint, then sole principal from at least 1810 and into the 1820s.

In 1814, Joshua established a coal works at Henllys, four miles north of Newport in Wales. This was in the early days of the South Wales coalfields, when relatively little capital was needed to set up a colliery business. Colliers owned the buildings and equipment, but they leased rather than bought the land, paying royalties to the landowner on the coal extracted. The growing demand for coal by other industries meant that mining was lucrative for both landowner and colliery owner.

By the 1840s, Hanson's coal works occupied more than 300 acres across the parishes of Henllys and Llantarnam. It included a tramroad (a small railway) linking the colliery to the Monmouthshire Canal, a colliery dock with at least nine canal boats, a stone quarry and a tin-plating works. Joshua's son, Cyrus,

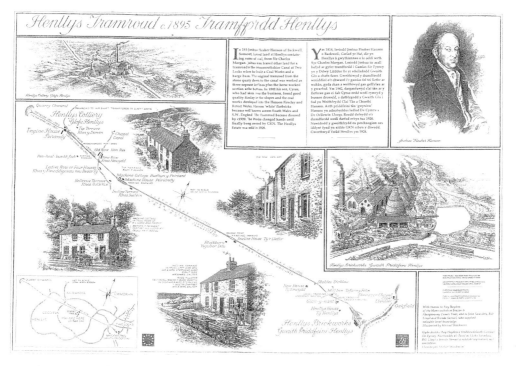

Illustrations by Michael Blackmore for an information board at the former site of Hanson's colliery, tramroad and brickworks at Henllys, Monmouthshire. Image supplied by Phil Jenkins of Industrial Gwent. Reproduced with kind permission of the Blackmore family.

The information at the top of the board states, in English and Welsh:

In 1814, Joshua Flesher Hanson of Backwell, Somerset, leased land at Henllys containing seams of coal from Sir Charles Morgan. Joshua also leased other land for a tramroad to the Monmouthshire Canal at Two Locks where he built a Coal Works and a barge basin. The original tramroad from the stone quarry down to the canal was worked as three separate inclines plus the horse worked section at the bottom. In 1842 his son, Cyrus, who had taken over the business, found good quality fireclay in the slopes and the coal works developed into the Hanson Fireclay and Retort Works. Hanson 'white' firebricks became well known across South Wales and S. W. England. The tramroad became disused by c. 1920. The works changed hands until finally being owned by GKN. The Henllys Estate was sold in 1928.

17

joined the business and discovered that the site contained seams of clay. Cyrus added a brickworks producing high quality firebricks, much in demand for constructing furnaces, kilns and fireplaces.

Joshua was an active member of the business community in South Wales, although he seems not to have lived there: the family had a home in Backwell, Somerset, across the Bristol Channel from Newport. He was elected a commissioner of Newport Harbour in 1836 and joined other local colliers in providing financial support to local churches and chapels. He supported charities in London, too, including the *London Asylum for the Support and Education of the Deaf and Dumb Children of the Poor* (a groundbreaking institution at the time, later becoming the *Royal School for Deaf Children* in Margate) and the *London Missionary Society*.

As well as his colliery and the Little Tower Street Academy, Joshua was a partner in at least two London businesses in the 1820s: a wholesale tea dealership and a dry-salter's, dealing in dyes and food preserving chemicals. But in 1818, at the age of 36, he had taken his first step into residential property development, with Regency Square.

The birth of Regency Square

Adevelopment such as Regency Square was a major undertaking. The developer needed land on which to build, money to lay down facilities such as roads and drains, as well as people willing and able to buy the new properties. It helped if he was already a builder or landowner, especially in Brighton, where the pattern of land ownership surrounding the old town was so complex. Since Joshua Flesher Hanson was neither landowner nor builder, his first task in creating Regency Square was to buy back his father's land.

Buying the land

When Francis Hanson's financial difficulties became insurmountable, all of his Brighton land apart from Belle Vue House was taken over by a group of creditors led by his son-in-law, John Austin. The takeover had been in December 1813, but Austin was still in control of the land when, in March 1818, Joshua Flesher Hanson bought it all back.

Joshua paid £4,435 for the 13 acres[9] his father had bought in the West Laine. The deal included the wharf, and Belle Vue's coach house and stables, but not Belle Vue House itself. The indenture (contract) confirming the sale includes a plan of the 13 acres and neighbouring properties.

At some point between 1818 and 1820, Joshua also bought a narrow strip of land immediately north of the 13 acres. We believe that this strip, which was probably purchased from Thomas Read Kemp, provided the land for Regency Mews.

It is surprising that Francis Hanson's land was still in the possession of his creditors after more than four years. It would have made sense for them

---

9   Not modern acres.

to try and recover the money they were owed, either by selling the land or developing it. So why had they not done this?

For that matter, why had Francis Hanson himself bought so much land and done nothing with it apart from building Belle Vue House, a coach house and stables?

An earlier development plan

In fact, Francis Hanson, possibly at the instigation of John Austin, had initiated a development scheme. In 1810, he had hired a surveyor called John Restall to draw up plans for a seafront square. But the scheme struggled, almost certainly because Britain was in the midst of the Napoleonic Wars (1803–1815). People who would normally invest in such developments were either strapped for cash – the Government had introduced Income Tax to help fund the war effort – or were patriotically lending their money to the Government. This left less cash available for investing in building developments. In any case, the threat of invasion probably made developments on the south coast look like a poor bet. Consequently, when building plots in Hanson and Restall's development were put up for sale by auction in 1811, there were no buyers.

Francis Hanson's was not the only local scheme to lie fallow. Work on Russell Square – Regency Square's immediate neighbour – and Bedford Square had started in the early 1800s, but Bedford Square was not completed until 1818 and few buildings were erected in Russell Square until the mid-1820s.

The first house

One of the plots in Restall's plan had eventually sold, in April 1813. It was bought by Mrs Sarah Street, and was a *piece of ground containing 21 feet in front and 89 feet in depth and described in a plan in the possession of John Restall…being one building plot part of the lawn and one in front of Preston Street on the west of the said lawn*. In other words, the plot was for two houses, one facing *the lawn* and another, at the rear, facing Preston Street, then little more than an outline.

The contract states that the house Mrs Street builds on the plot must have iron railings, 4ft 6ins high, at the front. It describes how she would have the right to walk on the lawn, provided she shared the cost of its upkeep with owners of other houses fronting the lawn. She was also required to pay towards making the roads and footpaths in the square.

Mrs Street died in January 1814, but her will suggests that building work on the house had already begun. She left the plot to her daughter, Mrs Sarah Jane Sim. It features in the plan of the land Joshua purchased in 1818, as well as in an 1819 plan of the Regency Square lawn. Its position is No. 7 Regency Square.

We can't be sure that No. 7 as it appears today is as built by Mrs Street or Mrs Sim. It's possible that it was a subsequent owner who completed the house, or that the front of the house was altered to resemble its new neighbours.

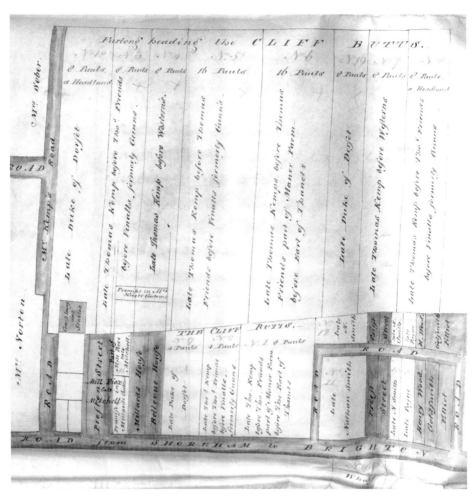

Plan of the '13 acres' formerly owned by Francis Hanson and bought by Joshua Flesher Hanson in March 1818. The Hanson land is divided into plots indicating their size in pauls and their previous owners. Owners of neighbouring plots are also named. The bottom part of the plan shows plots in the Cliff Butts, the top part shows plots in the Furlong Heading the Cliff Butts. Shaded areas indicate roads and existing buildings.

Mr Kemp's Road, on the far left, marks the border between two furlongs, which means it was an ancient track. Francis Hanson's coach house and stable, the only buildings included in the sale, are beside this road (re-named Little Preston Street in April 1831). Also identified are Belle Vue House, the Mill Piece (former site of the West Mill), Mrs Street's plot (a little to the north of Belle Vue House) and the wharf (bottom right). The large plot next to the wharf and marked Late Nathan Smith became the site of 67 to 69 Regency Square and 84 Kings Road.

BH/G/2/1579. Courtesy of East Sussex Record Office at The Keep.

The source of the money

Since Francis Hanson's wealth had diminished and Joshua Flesher Hanson had become a successful collier, it is likely that the money for launching the Regency Square development came from coal.

Another possibility is that funds came from family members, including Joshua's wife and in-laws. Joshua had married Nancy Swaine in 1808 at the church of St Margaret Pattens in the City of London. In those days, any money or property a woman owned automatically became her husband's.

The Swaines were London hop merchants. Two of Nancy's relatives, John Swaine and Henry James Swaine, were certainly involved in some of the Regency Square development deals.

The naming of Regency Square

Joshua Flesher Hanson's first task after buying the land would have been to lay out a plan for the square. He may have resurrected John Restall's plan as a starting point. Unfortunately, no copies of the plan for either Regency Square or Restall's earlier scheme appear to have survived.

On 21 December 1819, Joshua signed a deed poll[10] declaring the *appointment of an estate*, 229ft wide and 490ft deep, part of which was *laid out as a lawn in the centre of a square to be called Regency Square*. These dimensions relate to the open spaces in the middle of the square: the lawn, the encircling road and the footpaths.

Hanson was already selling building plots in the square. The deed poll clarifies that, in permitting future householders to use the lawn, roads and footpaths, he was not relinquishing ownership of these spaces. The deed poll is accompanied by a plan showing the position of the lawn and the first few houses under construction.

---

10 A deed poll is a legal document in which a person declares an intention. It is probably most familiar in the context of a person changing their name.

The deed poll is not the first time the name Regency Square is mentioned.[11] The name of the square was appearing in contracts for building plots from at least June 1819.

---

11 The History of Brighton and Environs by Henry Martin, 1871, states that Regency Square was originally to be called Waterloo Square. Martin may have had access to documents that have since been lost, but the only surviving evidence of an alternative name is a map published in 1822 by Wetton & Jarvis. This shows Regency Square as *Waterloo Square*, but it is an error: *Regency Square* was already in common use by 1822, appearing in newspapers in 1821, in Belch's map of 1822 and Baxter's 1822 street directory.

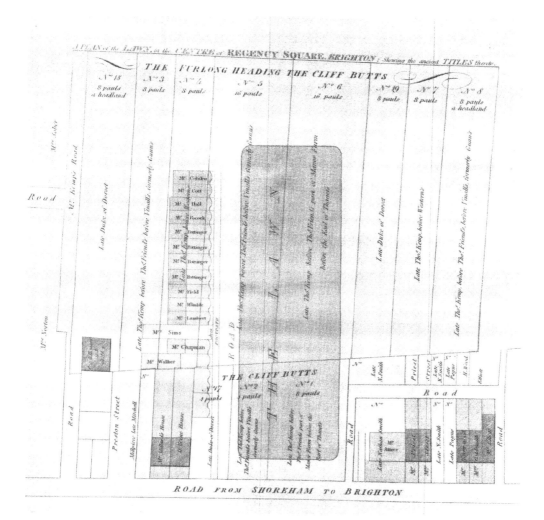

A Plan of the Lawn in the Centre of Regency Square, Showing the Ancient Titles thereto. Part of the 1819 deed poll in which Hanson declared his ongoing ownership of the open spaces in the centre of the square.

The main purpose of the plan is to show the position of the lawn. It also shows the first few houses under construction and the plot sold to Mrs Sarah Street in 1813, now owned by her daughter, Mrs Sim. The surveyor who drew the plan is not identified.

SAS/BRI/18 Courtesy of East Sussex Record Office at The Keep.

Building begins

In the summer of 1819, a Brighton builder called Shadrach Pocock leased a plot on the west side of Regency Square. It was *the eleventh plot from the north end of Belle Vue garden wall.* The plots for Nos. 1 to 4 Regency Square lay along the eastern boundary of Belle Vue, so the *eleventh plot from the north end* of Belle Vue is No. 15 Regency Square.

Pocock would be allowed to buy the plot outright, for £245, if he built the carcass of a house within nine months. Either way, he had to complete the entire house, at his own expense and *in a proper and workmanlike manner,* within two years. Failure to meet the deadlines meant Pocock would forfeit the plot and Hanson would repossess it.

The front of the house was to face the lawn and be built according to a design signed off by both Hanson and Pocock. Unfortunately, a copy of the design has not survived and the contract does not name an architect.

The agreement with Pocock is the earliest surviving example of how Hanson developed the square. The terms of Pocock's deal are echoed in all subsequent agreements. They include a set of building conditions and a set of covenants. The covenants laid down owners' and occupiers' ongoing obligations for maintaining the appearance of the houses and the character of the square.

Shadrach Pocock met the deadline for completing the carcass of the house and bought the freehold in June 1820. The house was more or less completed by April 1821, when he sold it to a well-known Brighton man, Mr James Robison, for £1,400. Pocock had not yet finished the painting and wallpapering, so Robison withheld the money until the house was ready for him to move in.

Pocock must have found the venture profitable, because in the spring of 1822 he leased another building plot in the square: No. 63 on the east side. The price for this plot was £441, the higher price reflecting its larger size: 21ft wide and 90ft deep, against No. 15's 19ft 6ins x 60ft. The terms were the same as for No. 15, except that this time the front of the house, rather than the carcass, had to be completed within nine months. As before, the front elevation had to match an agreed design.

No. 63 may have presented Pocock with some cash flow problems, because Hanson lent him £300, secured on the property, for a few months in 1822. But Pocock was able to sell the house in December that year, to Mr Isaac Newton Wigney.[12] The house was even less finished than when he had sold No. 15: he was still in the process of installing fireplaces and railings.

Who were the builders?

Original documents relating to building 28 of the houses – more than a third of the total – have survived. In half of these, a local builder leased the plot, building the house at his own expense and selling it as soon as it was completed.

Some local builders, like Shadrach Pocock, built more than one of Regency Square's houses in this way: Shadrach Pocock built Nos. 15 and 63; John Field built Nos. 9 and 10; Benjamin Tuppen built Nos. 52 and 56. Other local builders leasing plots were John Chalcraft (No. 11), James Cott (No. 36), Moses Vine (No. 53), Henry Hollingdale (No. 54), William Field (No. 61), Thomas Pocock (No. 67) and Thomas Saunders (No. 68).

In other cases, local businessmen leased plots and paid to have a house built, either for their own use or as a speculative investment: Brighton brewer George Wigney leased the plot for No. 60 and hired local builder Joseph Field to build the house; William Saunders, a stationer, had the house at No. 66 built; Benjamin Ginn, a surveyor, had No. 55 built; local upholsterers Nicholas Johnson and Joseph Garbutt had No. 59 built.

Thomas Attree, an important local figure in Brighton, leased the plots of No. 69, in the south-eastern corner of the square, and the next door plot at 84 Kings Road. He used the two plots to build a pair of linked houses but is not known to have lived there himself.

---

12 Isaac Newton Wigney was later elected MP of Brighton, first in 1832 and again in 1841.

Other plots were sold to wealthy Londoners who had houses built, either for their own use or to sell or let: Thomas Walker had Nos. 3, 4 and 5 built, subsequently keeping No. 5 for his own use; John Mortlock bought at least five plots on the north and east sides of the square, keeping No. 51 for his own use. A London surveyor called William Mackie leased and built No. 65.

Variations in the building agreements

Shadrach Pocock's agreement stipulated that he must build the carcass of a house within nine months of leasing the plot of No. 15. Most of the other surviving contracts stipulate a deadline for completing the front elevation. The deadlines for these varied from six to 15 months.

These variations were probably driven by practical considerations. When Pocock began building No. 15, both of the neighbouring plots were vacant, so he had to build all four walls. As the square progressed, more of the builders would be starting when at least one of the party walls was already in place or under construction.

Some of the building plots on the west side of the square came with the option of building a second property at the rear, facing Preston Street.

Building materials

The agreements stipulated that the upper storeys of the front elevations were to be built with yellow brick or mathematical tiles. Bare brick was fashionable at this time, because brick was expensive: ordinary bricks cost 5s 4d per hundred in the early 1820s, the same price as an ounce of silver. Brick was expensive because it was in great demand and because it was taxed. Bare brick, especially *best yellow bricks*, therefore displayed the householder's wealth and status.

Mathematical tiles gave the impression of a brick built structure but they were hung from timber supports. It's not known if any of the Regency Square builders opted for tiles rather than brick.

The agreements laid down other rules about the fronts of the houses but none concerning the rest of the building. Not surprisingly, builders used a cheaper material, bungaroosh, for the rear, basement and party walls.

Bungaroosh is a composite of flint, broken brick and lime mortar. It is local to Brighton and other towns near the South Downs. A bungaroosh wall is built up in layers between timber shuttering. Unrendered bungaroosh walls at the back of some Regency Square houses can still be glimpsed from Regency Mews and Preston Street.

The footpaths around Regency Square were to be made with Chailey brick. There is a brickworks at Chailey to this day, but Sussex had many other brickworks, including in the area immediately to the west of Brighton. Other materials that could be sourced locally include the flint for bungaroosh, lime, cement and plaster, and iron from foundries in Brighton and Lewes.

Some construction materials – slate, glass, lead for pipes and roofs, structural timber – came from farther afield but, whether locally sourced or not, it all had to be transported to the site. Materials from distant sources will have arrived by sea to Shoreham harbour. Some may have journeyed all the way by sea, unloading at Hanson's wharf.

Building conditions for houses in Regency Square

The upper storeys to be built with the best yellow bricks or mathematical tiles.

The underside of the balcony to be covered with roman cement or mastic of one uniform stone colour.

The string course and cornice to be covered with roman cement or mastic or made of Portland Stone.

No bow to project more than 3ft from the front line.

No part of the balcony to project more than 2ft 6ins from the front of the house.

The height of the ground floor above ground level to be regulated by Joshua Flesher Hanson's surveyor.

Costs of party walls to be shared with the neighbouring builders.

No other building except appropriate offices to be erected on the plot.

The builder may form a 6ft 6ins wide (basement) area beyond the front line of the house on condition that it is enclosed with 4ft 6ins high iron railings set into a proper stone curb. The design of the railings to be decided by Joshua Flesher Hanson.

Coal vaults and cellars may be created under the footpath on condition that they are no more than the width of the footpath and are built with brick arches at least 9ins thick.

The builder must form the road and footpath in front of the house.[13] The road to be 30ft wide and made in a substantial manner. The footpath to be 9ft 6ins wide, made with Chailey bricks and a stone curb.

The owner or occupier may use the roads and footpaths in the square. This replaces the right to use any ancient roads or paths associated with the land.

The owner may connect the house to the sewer but no privy soil or other offensive matter may be discharged into the sewer.

The owner or occupier may walk on the lawn so long as he pays a proportion of the costs of maintaining the fences and buys a key to the gate.

In the early versions of the building conditions, Hanson promised that the sewer would be built by the middle of 1820 and the lawn enclosed once the first 20 houses were built. Owners and occupiers would not have to pay anything towards maintaining the railings round the lawn until the railings were in place. The lawn's railings were to be 4ft 3ins high and made of iron. They were to have gates and lamp irons and be painted with three coats of *good white lead in oil*.

Hanson fulfilled his promise to build the sewer by mid-1820 and the railings round the lawn were in place by March 1822.

---

13 Forming the pavement outside newly built houses was a requirement across all of Brighton, not just in Regency Square.

Covenants for houses in Regency Square

Owners must:

Not alter the front elevation of the house.

Not cover the part of the front elevation built with yellow brick.

Insure the house against loss or damage by fire up to three quarters of the house value. If the house burns down or is damaged, it must be rebuilt according to the original plan so as to range uniformly with the adjoining houses, *it being the intention to preserve an uniformity in the buildings in the square.*

Not put a shop window in the front or use the house for any trade, business or calling whatsoever.

Not use the house in a manner likely to cause nuisance or injury to the neighbours.

Paint the outside wood and ironwork every three years with at least two coats of paint, the colour to be decided by the Regency Square committee, *in order that the fronts of the houses have an uniformity of appearance.*[14]

Pay a fair and equal proportion of the expenses, determined by the Regency Square committee, of maintaining the lawn and the roads around the square.

Pay a fair and equal proportion of the expenses of cleansing and repairing the sewers.

Not release any privy soil or other offensive matter into the sewer.

Hanson promised:

The lawn would *forever thereafter be used as a pleasure ground for the owners and occupiers of the houses* and would not be built on or converted to any purpose whatsoever.

Nothing would be built on the south side of the square that would reduce the space between the houses on the east and west sides to less than 229ft *it being the intent that a clear and uninterrupted view may be at all times preserved toward the sea.*

The covenants were to remain in place until Christmas Day 1889.

The Regency Square committee was to consist of Joshua Flesher Hanson (or, after his death, the owner of the central lawn) and four owners or occupiers of houses in the square, elected by the other owners or occupiers.

---

14 It was common for the woodwork of Georgian and early Victorian houses to be painted in a dark colour, imitating expensive wood. The fashion for painting woodwork in white or cream came later. Paint technology in the 19th century meant external ironwork may have been painted dark green or grey, but not black.

Regency-square
Sunday 11 August 1822

My dear Sister,
I told you that many of the houses round us were not finished. At first, I thought they were tumbling down. You can look right in though the empty windows and see all the workmen — carpenters, painters, bricklayers — all sorts. The pavement is not complete round the square yet, and oh! the mud when it rains. Even the road is not yet fully paved. When I go out, some of the men flirt a little with me and can be quite impudent. Do not mention that to Mother. The houses that are finished are grand, but they all look the same, which I think is very monotonous. On Monday there was a fire. It was caused by the plumbers who were repairing the lead of the gutter, right at the top of the house. They had left their irons heated during their dinner hour and these set the rafters alight. Mary said there was huge confusion and that the town engines were sent for. The firemen managed to put out the fire, but the roof was destroyed. What a terrible thing to happen — but it must have been exciting all the same. Don't tell Mother in case she worries.
Your loving sister
Polly

Building workers

Regency Square was far from being the only building development in Brighton in the 1820s, so craftsmen of all kinds – bricklayers, carpenters and joiners, plumbers, roofers, glaziers, plasterers – were in demand, as were general labourers. This meant that building materials were not the only imported resource.

Between 1811 and 1821, the population of Brighton doubled to over 24,000. By 1831, it had increased again to over 40,000. The growth was in part fuelled by people drawn to Brighton by the prospect of better paid work. The origins of working class migrants are difficult to identify until 1851, when the first census to record specific birth places was conducted. But anecdotal evidence from individual family histories identifies migrants from rural Sussex. Charles Martin, for example, who moved from Woodmancote to Brighton in the early 1820s to work as a bricklayer. The attraction of building work at that time was understandable. An agricultural labourer was paid an average 1s 9d a day (around £5 in today's money). On a building site, a general labourer would pocket 2s 3d (around £6.50) a day. Skilled craftsmen were better paid, at 3s 6d (around £10) a day.

The work was risky. In November 1821, a carpenter fell from one of the upper windows of a new house near Regency Square, dying at once from a broken neck. In June 1822, the scaffolding gave way on a house in Regency Square. Two men working on the scaffold fell 40ft, both of them breaking a leg, one of them also injuring his spine. A week later, a painter was seriously hurt when he fell from the scaffold of another house in Regency Square. Blame for the collapsed scaffolding was levelled at a labourer. It was said that he had caused the scaffold to give way by dropping a load of bricks.

The rapid rise of Regency Square

The construction of Regency Square began on the west side. The building plot for No. 7 had been sold in 1813, although the house may not have been completed until the 1820s. Other building plots between Nos. 3 and 18 were sold between 1819 and 1821, with most of these houses completed by 1822. Nos. 8 and 9 were advertised for sale in June 1821, when they were *on the eve of finishing*.

Most of the houses on the north and east sides of the square were begun in 1822, and at least half of them completed by 1824. Several completed houses on the north side – Nos. 23, 25 and 37 to 40 – were advertised for sale in the spring of 1823. Two unidentified *newly erected houses on the east side* were advertised for sale in August 1823.

The houses at the ends of the terraces were generally completed last. The exceptions were Nos. 67 to 69, at the seafront end of the east side. Building work on these houses began in 1819 and was complete by 1822. These three houses formed a block, separated from the rest of the square's east side by the road that would later become the exit from Queensbury Mews. The site is now occupied by a modern block of flats.

Baxter's 1822 street directory states there were 45 houses in Regency Square, but many of these will have been in various stages of construction. Occupied houses in Baxter's directory were mostly on the west side of the square. But by 1826, town rates were being collected from 58 of the eventual 71 houses in Regency Square.

Two superior well-built Freehold Residences, with bow fronts, five stories high, eligibly situate, and being Nos. 8 and 9, on the west side of Regency-square, Brighton, now on the eve of finishing, and of the annual value of £200 each, of which immediate possession may be had.

Particulars may be had of Messrs. Hill and Turner, solicitors, Brighton; Mr Meredith, solicitor, 8, New-inn-square, Lincoln's-inn; at Garraway's Auction Mart; and of Mr Mitchell, Norton-falgate, St. Martin's-le-Grand and Tottenham.

Morning Chronicle, 11 June 1821

BRIGHTON, SUSSEX

A desirable FREEHOLD ESTATE, situate in Regency Square.

TO BE SOLD BY AUCTION

By Mr. Shotter

At the "Ship in Distress Inn," Middle-Street, on Thursday, March 27, 1823, at seven o'clock in the evening

That valuable well-built Freehold HOUSE, situate and being 25, Regency Square, comprising a housekeeper's room and underground kitchen, well fitted up with every office convenient, and yard. – First Floor – Two parlours, with folding-doors, private water-closets, and small garden behind. – Second Floor – An elegant drawing-room well fitted up with cornice and marble chimney-piece, with a veranda in front, and good bed-room behind. – Third Floor – Two good bed-rooms, with three good attics over.

For further particulars enquire of Mr. SHOTTER, Auctioneer, Appraiser, Estate, House and Commercial Agent, adjoining the Theatre, New Road, Brighton.

Sussex Advertiser, 24 March 1823

BRIGHTON, SUSSEX

Valuable Freehold property

TO BE SOLD BY AUCTION

By Mr. F. SHOTTER

At the "Ship in Distress Inn," at the Bottom of Middle-Street, on Thursday, March 27, 1823, at half-past seven o'clock in the evening

Lot 6 – A valuable new-built FREEHOLD HOUSE, situate & being No. 38, Regency-square: comprising a housekeeper's room, and underground kitchen, well fitted up with every office convenient, and yard; first floor – Two parlours, with folding-doors, private water-closet, and garden behind; second floor, an elegant drawing-room well fitted up with cornice &c. and viranda (sic) in front, and good bed rooms behind; third floor, two good bed rooms, with three good attics over.

For further particulars enquire of Mr. F. SHOTTER, Auctioneer, Appraiser, Estate, House and Commercial Agent, adjoining the Theatre, New Road, Brighton.

Sussex Advertiser, 24 March 1823

A significant landmark

The scale of the development at Regency Square meant it was a significant landmark long before building was complete. The Kentish Weekly Post reported smuggled spirits landed at *Regency Square* in 1821. The square barely consisted of a single terrace at that time.

Builders of other developments used their proximity to Regency Square as a selling point: *near Regency Square* (houses in Spring Street, 1823), *immediately connected with the Kings Road and Regency Square* (a house in Cannon Place, 1827) and *immediately adjoining that very desirable spot Regency Square* (houses in Russell Square, 1828).

Advertisements for houses in Regency Square itself described the square as *noble and fashionable* even while most of it was still a building site (1823).

> Two officers belonging to the Rottingdean Preventive Guard boarded a French lugger with a cargo of contraband spirits, on Wednesday night. The crew, consisting of six Frenchmen and one English sailor, refused to surrender, and stood out to sea. When 20 miles from the coast, the smugglers compelled the officers to get into the large tub boat of the lugger, and return to shore. At three o'clock the following morning, about 120 tubs (supposed to have been part of the cargo of the above lugger) were landed opposite Regency-square; 46 of which were seized by the Brighton officers, and deposited in the store in Black Lion-street. The tub-boat, in which the officers came ashore, with two tubs it contained, has been seized.
>
> *Kentish Weekly Post, 2 March 1821*

Progress slows

In 1825, a stock market crash led to a financial crisis in which many banks collapsed. That, in turn, caused a credit crunch, a tightening of bank lending that hindered investment in new developments. This is almost certainly why the last few properties in Regency Square were slow to be completed.

No. 7 was probably still unfinished in 1826, but completed no later than 1829, when the new owner applied for permission to construct coal vaults under the pavement.

No. 2 was completed by 1828. No. 1 was under construction in 1828, but no more than a carcass at the end of that year.

Work on Nos. 43 to 46 had begun by 1825 but the builders gave up before the houses were finished. The four plots were taken over by a Londoner, John Mortlock, who completed them in 1831.

Nos. 47 to 50 were completed by 1832.

No. 1, Regency Square, the mere carcass of a house, by Public Auction, was knocked down by Mr. Parsons, this day at the Royal York Hotel, to the bidding of £2,500. The ground plot on which it had been erected, was previously sold by the said Auctioneer, for twelve hundred guineas, its dimensions, 35ft. by 25 – being after the rate of about *seventy thousand guineas per acre.* Less than half a century ago, perhaps, the whole of the land which now bears the valuable property of Regency Square, might have been purchased for a few hundred pounds – the gratifying change has doubtless been produced by the patronage of his Majesty, and the consequent preference which nobility and fashion have given to Brighton.

Sussex Advertiser, 29 December 1828

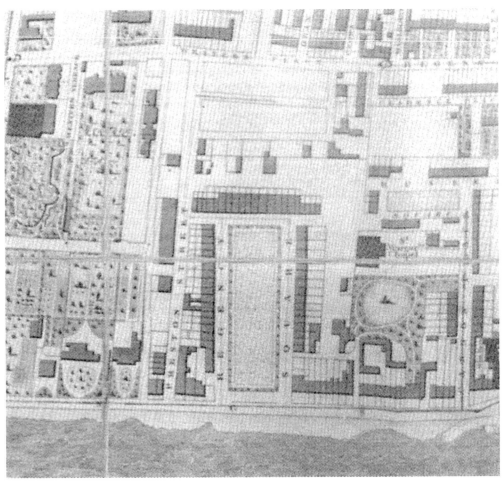

Extract of Pigot-Smith's 1826 map of Brighton, showing Regency Square. Nos. 1 and 2, and the north-eastern corner of the square are not yet built. The map is not wholly reliable, because Nos. 67 and 68 are also shown as blank spaces, but these are known to have been completed in 1822.

Courtesy of East Sussex Record Office at The Keep.

Design and architects

Regency Square was not the first of Brighton's seafront squares – work on Bedford Square had begun a few years earlier and New Steine was built in the 1790s – but it was the first of the large squares. The construction of Regency Square preceded that of Sussex Square and Lewes Crescent in Kemp Town, and of Brunswick Square and Adelaide Crescent in Hove.[15]

The ground plan

No ground plan for the whole square has survived, either in relation to Joshua Flesher Hanson's Regency Square or the earlier scheme, drawn up for Hanson's father by John Restall.

Joshua may have based Regency Square on Restall's plan, but the Restall scheme was for a smaller development. The combined frontage of houses with a sea view in Restall's development was *upwards of 700 feet*. The combined frontage of Regency Square houses with a sea view is over 1,200 feet.

Some anomalies in the early house numbering suggest that both plans had intended the square to be set further back from the seafront.

The building plot sold to Sarah Street in 1813 was *situated on the west side of the intended lawn…described in a plan in the possession of John Restall as No. 3*. Mrs Street's building plot is now No. 7 Regency Square, but it would have been *No. 3* if the first house in Restall's square was to have been built behind Belle Vue House, rather than alongside it.

---

15 Sussex Square and Lewes Crescent were begun in 1823, designed and built by the team of Wilds and Busby. Brunswick Square, designed by Charles Busby, was begun in 1824; Adelaide Crescent, designed by Decimus Burton, in 1830.

When Shadrach Pocock sold his newly built house to James Robison in 1821, the contract described it as No. 14, but the house is in fact No. 15. Was this an error in the 1821 contract? Or is it an indication that Joshua initially intended No. 1 Regency Square to be the most southerly house facing the lawn, rather than the seafront corner house?

Shadrach Pocock's first contract, in June 1819, promised 109ft of open space between the east and west sides of the square. Subsequent contracts, for houses on the north and east sides, promised 229ft of open space. Another error? Or evidence that Joshua changed his mind about the scale of the square after building had begun?

Overall design

The building covenants repeatedly emphasise the importance of the square maintaining a uniform appearance. Yet there are variations in the design of the individual houses. Variations, for example, in the number of storeys: within the same terrace, there are buildings of three, four and five storeys. Variations, too, in whether the houses have bow fronts.

Some aspects of the design of the houses are due to the orientation of the square. The south-facing houses in the middle of the north side have less need of bow windows, whose main purpose in a seafront development is to provide a better view of the sea, as well as allowing more light into the rooms.

Practical issues meant that the dimensions of the building plots varied. At the southern end of the west side, the building plots for Nos. 2 to 4 were laid out alongside the garden wall of Belle Vue House. These building plots were therefore broader and shorter than others in the square, and this explains why these houses are double fronted.

Only one other house in Regency Square, No. 43, has a double frontage. In this case, it's because one half of the ground floor incorporated a carriage entrance to the mews behind.

In spite of the variations, each of the square's three sides was clearly constructed with an overall design in mind. The north side of Regency Square is symmetrical. The middle of the terrace has a *palace front*, designed

Regency Square in 1860
Courtesy of the Society of Brighton Print Collectors and the Regency Society

to appear as a single, palatial building. It is flanked by matching pairs of bow fronted houses, then by further matching pairs of houses under ornamental pediments and finally by rows of similar houses to each end of the terrace. The symmetry of the north side is cleverly maintained by switching the position of the front doors, from left to right, in mid-terrace.

The upper section of the east side – north of the Queensbury Mews exit – is also symmetrical. Some of the detail in the front elevations has been lost but enough remains to see that there is a central group of houses, the middle one with a pediment, and a series of matching sets of houses, with and without pediments, on either side.

The west side – the first part of Regency Square to be built – has no palace front or pediments. But in the upper section, north of the double fronted houses, a central group of houses stands taller than the rest, with matching rows on either side.

*Nos. 11 to 14 Regency Square, from particulars of sale at auction, June 1826. Nos. 11 to 13
are the taller houses in the centre of the west side.
HOW 21/7 Courtesy of East Sussex Record Office at The Keep.*

The symmetry within each terrace implies an overall design. The use of pediments, pilasters and other ornamentation on the north and east sides, but not on the earlier west side, suggests that the design may have changed as work progressed. There was certainly a change of heart in the matter of porticos: most of the porticos on the west side have Doric columns, but those on the east side have Ionic columns. Nos. 2 to 4 use both on every doorway! Is it possible that, as building progressed, Hanson felt that the original design was not grand enough?

Who was the architect?

Architecture did not become a formal profession until the mid-19th century. Until then, the task of designing buildings was usually inseparable from the work of constructing them. Artisan builders, surveyors and developers could choose styles and design features from pattern books containing the necessary

Waterloo Place (near St Peter's Church), designed by Amon and Amon Henry Wilds.
James Gray Collection, Courtesy of the Regency Society

technical specifications. But the use of unifying features such as shared pediments and palace fronts indicates that Regency Square's appearance was influenced by someone we would nowadays call an architect.

The square shares similarities with other developments in Brighton from this period. Tall, narrow, bow fronted houses still stand in St George's Place and Richmond Terrace. A strikingly similar design to Regency Square's north terrace existed at Waterloo Place. These developments were built at the same time or shortly before Regency Square, and were the work of Amon Wilds and his son, Amon Henry Wilds. Amon Wilds was a builder-developer; his son's interests lay more in design.

There are other grounds for believing Regency Square's appearance to have been the work of the Wilds. The decorative pilasters on the central houses in the north and east terraces are typical Wilds features, as are the scallop shell designs at the tops of some of the pilasters.

Historic England (formerly English Heritage), the public body responsible for listing buildings[16], believes Regency Square was *probably* designed by the Wilds, but admits it has no documentary evidence of this. Only one building in the square is definitely known to have been designed by one of the Wilds: No. 1 Regency Square, now the Regency Restaurant and renumbered 131 Kings Road, was designed by Amon Henry Wilds. Among this building's features are the scallop shells seen elsewhere in the square.

All contracts and agreements for building the Regency Square houses state that the front elevation had to conform to an agreed design. Two of the designs have survived, in both cases for houses on the east side: Nos. 59 and 69. These designs bear the signatures of Hanson and the individuals who had leased the plots. The signatures are witnessed by William Mackie. On the design for No. 69, his witnessing signature reads *William Mackie Architect, Charlotte Street, Blackfriars Road.*

Mackie was a London surveyor, hired by the Brighton town commissioners to build the workhouse behind St Nicholas' Church in 1821–22. He leased the plot for No. 65 Regency Square in 1822 and built this house, selling it as soon as it was complete in 1823, then leasing it back again, to live in or sub-let. His name also features as a party to one other contract and a witness to several – but not all – documents concerning the construction of houses on the east side between 1820 and 1823. It doesn't feature on any of the surviving documents relating to houses on the north and west sides of the square.

Did Mackie witness these documents because he designed the houses on the east side of the square? Witnesses to other contracts and documents were usually solicitors or, occasionally, Hanson's relatives or business associates. In witnessing the design for No. 69, Mackie gives his occupation and address, but it's the only time he does so. If he was the architect of the east terrace, did he copy the style of the Wilds and was this because the Wilds were responsible for other parts of the square? Unfortunately, no trace of Hanson's correspondence with architects has been found, so this remains a matter for conjecture.

---

16 All but one of Regency Square's original houses are Grade 2 or Grade 2* listed. The war memorial and the bollards in the footpath to Russell Square are also listed.

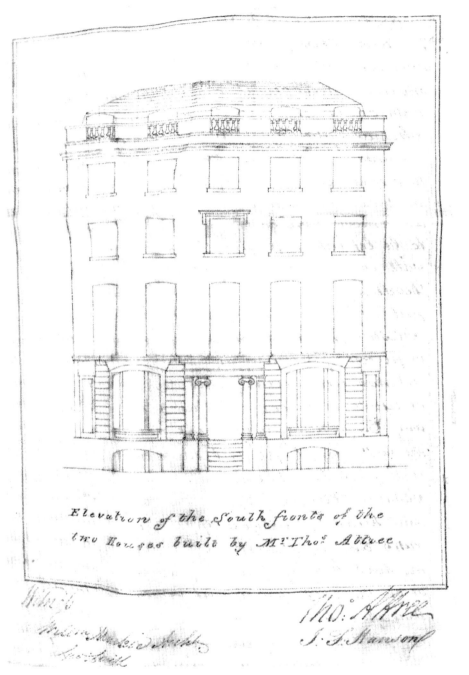

Plan of the front elevation, facing the seafront, of 69 Regency Square and 84 Kings Road, July 1820. Signed by Thos Attree and J. F. Hanson, signatures witnessed by William Mackie, architect. AMS 6717/1 Courtesy of East Sussex Record Office at The Keep.

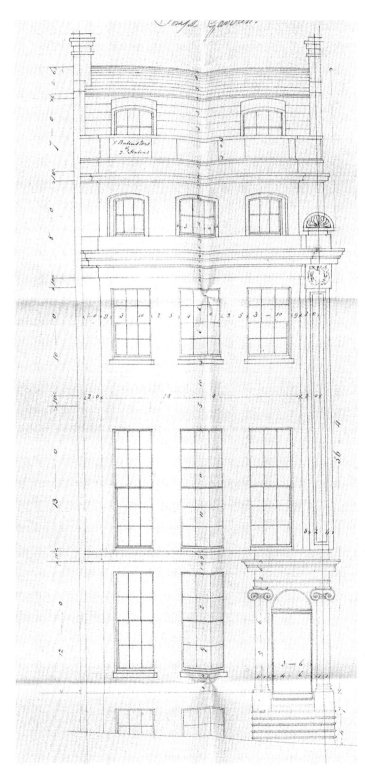

Plan of the front elevation of 59 Regency Square, May 1822, prepared for Messrs Johnson and Garbutt, witnessed by William Mackie. The shell ornamentation on the third floor does not feature on the house today and may not have been included when the house was built.

ACC 8767/1 Courtesy of East Sussex Record Office at The Keep.

The seafront corners

No. 1 Regency Square occupies the south-west corner and is very different in appearance from other houses in the square. Its appearance would have been even more out of step with the rest of the square but the builder, Amon Henry Wilds, was forced to amend the design during construction. Neighbours complained that the house projected into the square, obstructing the view from No. 2. The town commissioners insisted that it must be built in a line with the houses on either side.

The opposite, south-eastern corner, was occupied by No. 69. In common with No. 1, this corner house looked out onto the seafront as well as the square, but No. 69 was different in other respects: together with Nos. 67 and 68, it was separated from the rest of the square's east side by the exit road from Queensbury Mews. It was also inextricably linked to its seafront neighbour, then numbered 84 Kings Road.[17]

The building plots for 69 Regency Square and 84 Kings Road were both leased from Joshua Flesher Hanson by Thomas Attree. The two houses were designed to look like a single prestigious property.

Nos. 67 and 68 were built to the same design as No. 69 – implying that the same architect was responsible for all three – including an unusual ornamental lintel above the windows in the centre of the second storeys. These lintels also feature, and can still be seen, on the double fronted houses opposite, Nos. 2 to 4. Houses on the south and west sides of Russell Square (designed by Amon Henry Wilds) have similar lintels on their upper storeys.

Today, the entire site of 67 to 69 Regency Square and 84 Kings Road is occupied by a modern block of flats.

---

17 All seafront buildings west of East Street were given Kings Road addresses at the end of the 1830s. This meant renumbering those houses with existing Kings Road addresses and giving entirely new addresses to others. The house formerly known as 84 Kings Road became 129 Kings Road. Regency Square's seafront corner houses, No. 69 and No. 1, became 130 and 131 Kings Road. Confusion over the renumbering persisted for years. In the 1850s, street directories included the south-west corner house twice in each edition, as 1 Regency Square and as 131 Kings Road; directories continued to identify the south-east corner as 69 Regency Square until the early years of the 20th century.

*69 Regency Square and 84 Kings Road showing
two front doors. Detail from The Brighton Panorama 1834
Courtesy of Royal Pavilion & Museums, Brighton & Hove*

No. 1: St Albans House

In 1815, the successful actress, Harriot Mellon married Sir Thomas Coutts, one of the richest men in England. Sir Thomas died in 1822, leaving his wife one of the wealthiest widows in England. Five years later, Mrs Coutts married the young William Aubrey de Vere Beauclerk, ninth Duke of St Albans, one of the many descendants in England of Charles II and Nell Gwyn. The age discrepancy in the first marriage was 42 years and in the second a mere 24.

Even before their marriage, the widow and the peer were spoken of in the same column inches. In 1824, *The Duke of St Albans, Lord Burford and the Ladies Beauclerk, have become the occupants of Belle Vue House. Mrs Coutts and family are expected to take possession of Byam House on the King's-road on Monday.* Byam House (Cavendish House in 2018) was just 120 yards from Belle Vue House.

Once they were married, the noble couple set about acquiring No.1 Regency Square, then in the early stages of construction. It became known as St Albans House.

The Duke and Duchess of St Albans were regularly lampooned in cartoons and criticised in the press. The Duchess in particular was an early victim of contemporary paparazzi.
© *National Portrait Gallery, London*

By the early 1830s the couple were visiting the town regularly and in January 1832 they *entertained a brilliant party of about two hundred people with a ball and a supper at St Alban's House in Regency-square.* In January 1833 *the Duchess of St Albans had a Quadrille Party last evening at St Alban's House.* A month later there was another party for 200 people: *Dancing commenced, to Behrne's band, at half-past 10, and the company departed shortly after three.* Probably much to the displeasure of the neighbours. The Brighton correspondent of one London paper even ascribes to the happy couple *the revival of the gaieties of the place.*

Did the couple ever own the house? It is not sure. Despite St Albans House frequently being referred to as *their Graces' residence*, as with so many of the Regency Square houses, this was a property to let. Newspapers reported that *The Duke and Duchess have taken St Alban's House till the beginning of …*, or that *The Duchess has re-engaged St Alban's House for two months*, while also reporting that *Mr X has arrived and taken possession of the splendid mansion at the corner of Regency-square called St Alban's House*, or that *Mr Y, the banker has taken St Alban's House*. On the other hand, perhaps it was the noble couple who let out the property to other visitors – of the most genteel class, of course.

By late 1834, the St Albans were spending large amounts of cash on improving No.1 Regency Square – or at least on the stables. These were in Little Preston Street and had been the coach house and stables of Belle Vue House. A riding school had been added in 1828.

> The Duke and Duchess of St. Alban's, for whom apartments had been engaged at the Bristol, have determined on prolonging their stay in the Isle of Wight until St. Alban's House, at the corner of Regency Square, shall become vacant. In their stables, the large circle under the dome has been paved, and the uniformity of the surface make it appear to have been enlarged; a gas lamp has been placed over every stable door, and one of enlarged dimensions crowns the handsome cast iron pillar which stands in the centre of the cistern. In a word, the tout ensemble of the unrivalled establishment has been so much improved as to excite the surprise of those who were before conversant with its imposing appearance. The riding school attached to the stables is, with the exception of Westminster Abbey, the largest room in England whose roof is not supported by pillars and the dome which surmounts the stables is only inferior to that of St. Paul's in circumference.
>
> *Sussex Advertiser 6 October 1834*

Over the course of their many sojourns at St Albans House, the couple hosted *déjeuners, fêtes,* balls, a public breakfast, not to mention a lunch *à la fourchette.* However, the most curious sight for the residents of Regency Square must have been the Duke of St Albans in his uniform as the Grand Falconer of England. The hereditary post of Grand Falconer was not merely nominal as far as the Duke was concerned. He frequently gave displays of falconry near the Devil's Dyke and he *put his hawks in the Regency Square enclosure very frequently. They attracted considerable attention.*

The couple's enjoyment of their residence was short lived. In January 1837, the Duchess was suffering from *the prevalent influenza* and a grand ball at St Albans House had to be cancelled. By August, the Duchess was dead.

In the 180 years since then, St Albans House has gone through three main phases. Until the turn of the 20th century it was a lodging house. At this point, the ground floor was lowered and remodelled for retail use when Lawson and Sons, Jewellers moved in. They occupied the ground floor, with flats or rented rooms above, until WW2 when Brighton was very exposed to attack. The seafront would not have been a good spot to trade in diamonds and pearls. A number of catering establishments followed, such as the short-lived China Doll Restaurant in 1954 and Tony's Café in the 60s and 70s, along with Rooky's Club from the mid-50s until early in the 1970s. Since then, the ground floor of St Albans House has had the good fortune to be home to the Regency Restaurant, the upper floors continuing to be residential.

St Albans House, 1 Regency Square in the 1930s. The building to the left is the former Belle Vue House.
Courtesy of Step Back in Time, Queens Road, Brighton

51

Abbotts

The block of flats standing at the south-east corner of Regency Square is called Abbotts. It was built in 1961/62 on the site of 67, 68 and 69 Regency Square, and 129 (formerly 84) Kings Road. By 1913, these houses had become Abbotts Hotel.

It is surprising that the Abbott name lives on, given the nature of the man who supplied it. James Vercoe Abbott was born in Deptford, Kent. As a young man he had been a commercial traveller. He was also a very successful *parliamentary agent*, moving around the country to work for different parliamentary candidates (Liberal and Conservative) in Ipswich, Ulverston, Falmouth, Brighton and Bournemouth.

He seemed to be a pillar of society: Freemason, Guardian of the Poor in Greenwich, highly respected member of the Ancient Order of Foresters, efficient organiser of ceremonial events and, in his later years, doughty critic of his local bishop's High Church stance. But did he have a darker side?

As the 19th century turned into the 20th, newspapers in Kent were questioning why Vercoe Abbott was so rarely at Guardians' meetings in Greenwich. He pleaded ill health, although he may also have been keeping clear of a Local Government Board inquiry (which he had championed) into possible corruption within the Greenwich Union Guardians. A 1907 article in The Times reports the inquiry's examination of matters at the Mile End Workhouse. Several of the workhouse suppliers had been wining and dining the Guardians, which was considered bribery. A representative for one supplier told the inquiry:

> *That applied not only to Mile-end but to Greenwich. He had met a man named Vercoe Abbott. … He dined with Abbott at Pinoli's, and after dinner lent him 30 shillings. That was all the money Abbott had from him, although he received a lot of silly letters from that person. He did not think it was worthwhile to go to the police and state that Abbott was blackmailing him.*

The 1911 census shows Vercoe Abbott running a boarding house (although still calling himself a parliamentary agent) in Montague Street just off Russell Square in London.

Having taken charge of Abbotts Hotel by 1913, Vercoe Abbott was declared bankrupt in 1914. In 1917 he was jailed for three months for smuggling margarine to France. He claimed he did not know it was illegal. In 1920 he took over the licence of the Station Hotel in Westgate-on-Sea where, a few months later, he was up before the court for overcharging on his bar prices.

James Vercoe Abbott died in Ipswich in 1928. His name is immortalised, seemingly undeservedly, on the south-east corner of Regency Square. But why was the original building demolished?

Firstly, it had been much altered over the years. In the mid-19th century, a monstrous chimney flue had been tacked on to the front of the building. Windows were enlarged and, in 1902, the seaward façade was rebuilt. This in turn was largely obscured by a massive sun lounge. There was little to indicate the original elegant lines of the property.

Abbotts Hotel 1920s (source unknown)

Demolition of Nos. 67 to 69 (Abbotts Hotel) Regency Square 1960
James Gray Collection, Courtesy of the Regency Society

Secondly, it was demolished in the 1960s, when historic buildings in central Brighton were being swept away in a frenzy of modernisation. The area now covered by Churchill Square, Kingswest and the Brighton Centre had been a maze of workshops, houses, tiny shops, elegant Georgian cottages and even a delightful farmhouse. The magnificent St Margaret's Church, to the east of Regency Square, had been razed to the ground in 1959. Whatever the historic or architectural merits of these buildings, the thinking at the time was that they had to go. On 6 December 1960, outline planning permission was granted to Brighton Residential Hotels Ltd for *the erection of a nine storey block of flats comprising 16 flats and basement car parking.*

The north-east corner

The north-east corner of Regency Square, Nos. 43 to 50, is a cul de sac, with a narrow footpath (*twitten* in local dialect) leading to Russell Square. It was the last part of the square to be completed. Some of the freeholds remained in the Hanson family's possession until the 1850s.

In 1861, the Regency Square management committee proposed renaming the north-east corner Regency Place. The proposal may have arisen because these had not originally been *privileged* houses, that is to say their occupants did not have access to the Regency Square lawn.

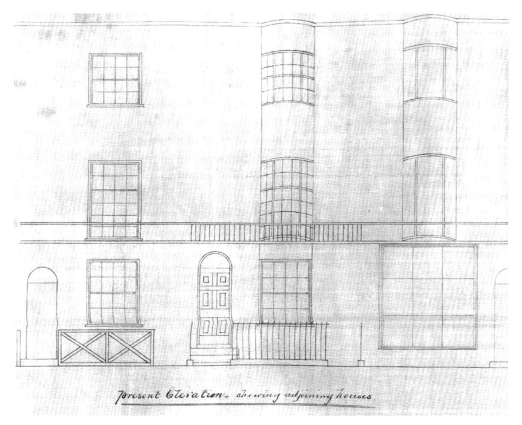

The 'present elevation' of Nos. 48 to 50 in October 1877, from the plan to replace the bow windows at No. 49. No. 47 also had bow windows until 1891.
DB/D 8/1720 Courtesy of East Sussex Record Office at The Keep

Nos. 43 to 46 Regency Square were completed in 1831. No. 43 was built with a carriage arch, an entrance to Regency Mews. The carriage entrance survived until 1997/8, when it was reconfigured to create a new apartment. Granite cobbles remain in the pavement, providing a lasting clue to the earlier feature.

Nos. 47 to 50, on the south side of the cul de sac, were built by 1832. They are often assumed to be mid-Victorian houses because they have angled bay windows. However, these windows are late 19th century alterations. When first built, three of the houses had bow windows, the fourth was flat fronted. A first floor balcony originally ran across all four houses.

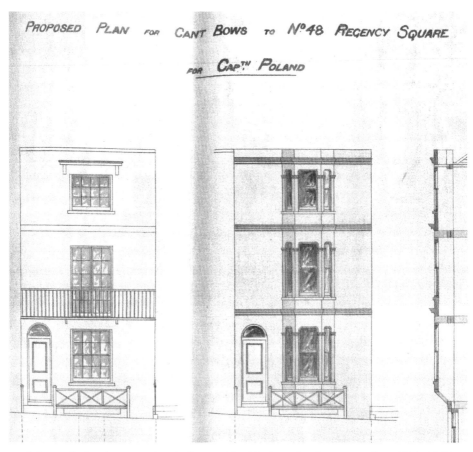

Before and after changes to the windows at No. 48, from the plan approved on 5 July 1888.
Captain Poland, the owner of the house, was master of the West Pier.
DB/D 8/3057 Courtesy of East Sussex Record Office at The Keep.

The bow windows at No. 49 were replaced with angled bays in 1877. Nos. 47 and 48 acquired bay windows a decade later.

The upper storey bay windows at No. 50 were installed in 1884, but the ground floor shop window is from an unknown earlier date.

No. 46a, at the entrance to the twitten, was built as a single storey architect's studio at the rear of 31 Russell Square. It first appears in directories as 46a Regency Square in 1864, continuing as an architect's practice until the mid-1890s. The opening credits of the 1948 film Brighton Rock include a glimpse of 46a, at that time still a single storey building, from the twitten. It is understood to have acquired its upper storey in the 1960s.

Scene from the opening credits of Brighton Rock showing the single storey 46a in 1948. Courtesy of STUDIOCANAL Films Ltd.

The unusual corner house between the Regency Tavern and No. 47 is nowadays No. 46b, but until the 1890s it was 46½. It was also known, until the 1990s, as Regency Cottage.

An 1855 auction advertisement describes the property as having *just been rebuilt in a substantial and ornamental manner by Messrs Field from the design of a London architect*. We don't know why it was rebuilt or what it had looked like before.

The rebuilt property was leased to Mr Edward Jordan, who briefly ran it as a dairy. We assume that it was a dairy in the sense of selling milk, butter, cream and cheese, not that Mr Jordan milked cows on the premises. The ghost of Jordan's name was revealed, sign-painted above the door, during repainting in 2014.

The ornate upper storeys of 46b have filled the corner of the cul de sac since at least 1855, but the ground floor has done so only since 1980. Previously, the front door and ground floor window were set back from the street and a narrow passage ran under the first floor of the house, originally to St Margaret's Church. The church, whose main entrance was in St Margaret's Place, was demolished in 1959 and replaced by Sussex Heights. The Regency Cottage end of the passage remained, as a store room, until the front door was remodelled in 1980.

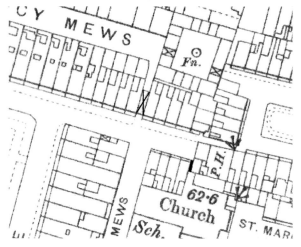

Extract from 1911 Ordnance Survey map showing the north-east corner of Regency Square. The elongated cross on the property between the upper and lower mews marks the carriage entrance at No. 43. The narrow passage to St Margaret's Church is indicated as a thick black line. P.H. is the Regency Tavern, then occupying only two of the properties in the twitten.

Courtesy of Ordnance Survey.

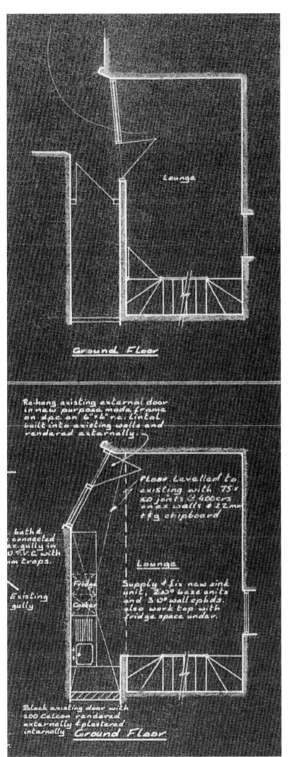

Extract from the blueprint of 46b, before and after the remodelled front door. The 'before' version, top, shows the recessed front door and the remains of the passage to St Margaret's Church at the side of the house. The 'after' version, bottom, shows the repositioned front door at its present angle, the remains of the passage absorbed into the house.

DB/D 139/79/3/3310 Courtesy of East Sussex Record Office at The Keep.

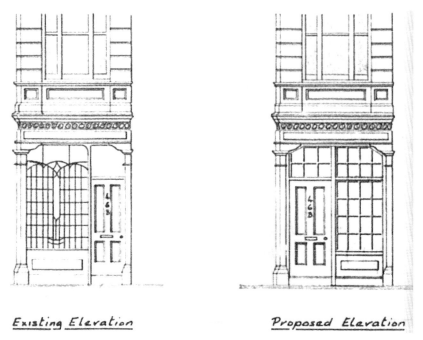

Existing Elevation   Proposed Elevation

Before and after plan of the entrance to 46b, 1979. What is not obvious from the 'before' drawing is that the front door and ground floor window were set back from the upper storeys. DB/D 139/79/3/3310 Courtesy of East Sussex Record Office at The Keep.

Still from Brighton Revisited, 1969, Joseph Cantor, showing 46b's recessed ground floor frontage. Reproduced by kind permission of Screen Archive South East

Regency Colonnade

The twitten to Russell Square was built as part of the Regency Square development. It was originally called Regency Colonnade, but the name was lost in the 1870s, when the properties were renumbered as part of Russell Square.

Today, the twitten is occupied by the Regency Tavern, but this was built as three separate premises. The earliest record of these premises is in April 1829, when the pavement was laid in front of them.

In November 1830, the occupants asked the town commissioners to put posts at the entrance to the twitten in order to stop horses and hand carriages passing through. The following summer, the commissioners also approved adding a flight of steps to the twitten entrance.

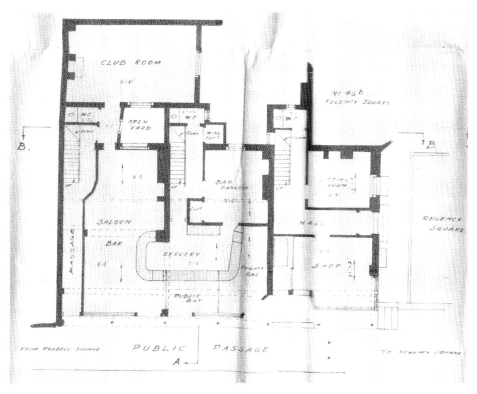

Ground floor plan of properties in the former Regency Colonnade, 1938. The Regency Tavern occupied the two properties at the Russell Square end. The property at the Regency Square end was still a separate shop, with an entrance facing the cul de sac.
PTS 2/9/696 Courtesy of East Sussex Record Office at The Keep.

In 1832, No. 1 Regency Colonnade, at the Regency Square end, was occupied by John Bax, a grocer; No. 2 by Mr Clarke, a beer retailer; and No. 3, at the Russell Square end, by John Dix, a carpenter. From 1839, No. 3 was variously an eating house and beer shop. In 1852 it was the Regency Coffee House, changing its name to the Regency Tavern a year or two later.

In the late 1860s, there were two pubs in Regency Colonnade: the Regency Tavern at No. 3 and the Colonnade Tavern at No. 2. They merged in the 1870s under the name Regency Tavern.

In 1893, the owner of No. 1 had a doorway cut into the side of the building so that its entrance was in the cul de sac rather than the twitten. The doorway remained until 1938, when Tamplins brewery acquired No. 1 and absorbed it into a remodelled Regency Tavern.

The proposed new door in the side of 32 Russell Square (formerly 1 Regency Colonnade), 1893. This is now the side of the Regency Tavern facing Regency Square. The drawing, and the 1938 ground plan, show steps at the side of the twitten. DB/D 8/3746 Courtesy of East Sussex Record Office at The Keep.

Rates

In addition to contributions to the upkeep of Regency Square's lawn, roads and sewer, householders paid the usual town rates. These paid for street lights, fire engines and law enforcement, maintaining sea defences and repairing the town's main thoroughfares, household rubbish collection and watering the streets to keep the dust down. There was also a separate rate to fund *relief of the poor* in the parish.

The amount a householder paid in town and poor rates was based on an assessment of the value of his house. Town and poor rates therefore provide a clue to the variations in size and grandeur of Regency Square's houses.

In 1826, the town rates paid by Regency Square householders ranged from £1 11*s,* for houses at the western end of the north terrace, to £5 11*s* for No. 58 in the middle of the east terrace. Houses in the north terrace's central palace front paid £4 13*s.*

By 1834, when all the houses in the square were complete, the most valuable house in the square was No. 1. This householder paid £4 13*s* 6*d* in poor rates that year. No. 58, now the second most valuable property, paid £3 8*s* 6*d*. At the other end of the scale, Nos. 47 to 50 each paid 9/-, while properties in Regency Colonnade paid between 11/- and 12*s* 6*d*.

Hanson's management of the development

Hanson's approach to the Regency Square development – leasing building plots, having builders shoulder the costs of construction and imposing strict deadlines for completion – meant that he did not bear all the financial risk. His terms were generous: builders paid only a peppercorn rent for the plots in the first year and Hanson often lent them the money to complete the house. He advanced the loans in stages, as the building work progressed. The loan to Moses Vine in April 1822, for the construction of No. 53, is typical. It also gives some clues about the process of construction:

Joshua Flesher Hanson hereby engages to advance to Moses Vine £550 as follows:

£50 when the joists of the ground and first floor are laid

£100 ditto second and third floor

£100 ditto fourth floor and when the roof is covered in

£100 when the sash frames are in and glazed, the cornice finished and the scaffold removed and the iron fence and stone steps to front and to the area and all the front is complete

£100 when the garret floor and the two floors below are laid and the battening to the whole house is done, the garrets and the two floors below are plastered and finished and all the stairs are up

£100 when the whole is finished

And Moses Vine hereby engages to give his promissory notes for any sums so advanced payable with interest at 5pc per annum on the 1st day of April 1823 and will also repay Joshua Flesher Hanson insurance on £550… and Joshua Flesher Hanson shall have a lien on the premises till the whole is repaid.

Not all the builders exercised the option to buy the building plot. In some cases, such as No. 36, the builder only ever leased the plot, selling the house as soon as it was finished, the buyer paying Hanson for the freehold. In a few cases, such as Nos. 47 and 48, Hanson did not succeed in selling the freeholds for several years after the houses had been completed.

Roads

The land on Brighton's West Laine was privately owned. The only routes on the West Laine were the seafront road to Shoreham and the traditional tracks along the boundaries of furlongs. If someone built a house, it needed to be near a route that he and his visitors were entitled to use. He could not simply walk or drive across his neighbours' lands to reach his property. Similarly, if a landowner decided to develop his land by building a street of houses, residents would need a route to and from the new street.

Hanson's development included a new road, Preston Street. But he owned only the lower half of the Preston Street we know today. The reason Preston Street reaches all the way from the seafront to Western Road is because Hanson came to an agreement with Thomas Read Kemp, who owned the land to the north of Hanson's. The agreement, in 1820, was to mutual advantage: new houses and streets were also being built on Kemp's land, and it suited both parties for their roads to link up and allow public access.

John Vallance

How much involvement did Hanson have in the development while building was in progress? He had a colliery in Monmouthshire and other business responsibilities in London. His family was in London: three of his children were baptised there during the construction of Regency Square. He can have been in Brighton only intermittently while building was underway.

Hanson had a local representative in Brighton: John Vallance, a brewer and member of an influential Brighton family. Vallance was a party to most of the surviving contracts and agreements relating to Regency Square's development. The documents refer to him as Hanson's trustee, implying that he looked after Hanson's affairs in his absence.

Other associates of Hanson also feature in some of the contracts: various members of the Swaine family are parties to some contracts, occasionally acting as Hanson's agents; William Budden, who was Hanson's partner in a London tea dealership, was a party to at least one contract. None of these associates were buying or leasing building plots, but it's possible that they might have been lending money to Hanson.

Enforcing the covenants

We know that Hanson was sometimes in Brighton during Regency Square's development, because in 1824 he wrote to Isaac Newton Wigney from an address in Regents Place.[18] Wigney was the owner of 63 Regency Square. Hanson took him to task for building a coach house and stables at the back of the house, and washing the carriage in Queensbury Mews. *As this is quite contrary to the agreement between myself and the various parties,* wrote Hanson, *I take the earliest opportunity of cautioning you on the subject and trust you will see proper to desist.*

This must have been the first time Hanson had become aware of breaches of the Regency Square covenants, because he added, *I should be very sorry for the first question that has arisen on such a subject in my transactions at Brighton to take place with yourself.*

In reality, some householders were breaching one of the covenants from very early on. The houses were not to be used for *any trade, business or calling whatsoever.* But Nos. 6 and 22 were advertised as schools in the early 1820s. In 1839, No. 9 was also advertised as a school, No. 13 as a boarding house, No. 50 was a bakery, and five surgeons and physicians were advertising from Regency Square addresses. Houses in the cul de sac, including No. 50, may have always been exempt from the restriction concerning business use. But an 1841 lease for No. 9 indicates that the restriction had been relaxed for certain businesses and professions: the ban no longer applied to schoolmasters, surgeons, apothecaries and boarding houses.

---

18 Regents Place was the original name of the stretch of Western Road between North Street and Marlborough Street.

Once the square was complete, Hanson needed little ongoing involvement in its affairs. The covenants left decisions about external colour schemes, and the maintenance of the lawn and shared facilities, to a committee of residents. Hanson was a member of the committee, but we don't know how personally involved he remained.

Regency-square
Sunday 25 August 1822

My Dear Sister,
I haven't told you about this huge house yet. When I
arrived, the first person I met was Mary, the house
maid. She seems nice enough. Can you believe she is
only thirteen! She showed me up to my room. Although
it is so big, the house has only one set of stairs, so we
are allowed to walk on lovely soft carpets as far as the
third floor. From there, you open a little door and up
some narrow wooden stairs to the top floor where I have
my tiny room. Mary has a room next to mine. Ellen
the scullery maid sleeps by the kitchen range on a bed
she makes up at night. That's one of her few pieces of
luck. I have a little tiny fireplace but we are allowed coal
only on Sundays, so in the winter we were very cold at
night. There's always hot water from the kitchen boiler
but one job I really do not like is carrying hot water up
to the second floor for the Mistress morning and evening! I haven't told you about Mrs Drew, the cook. She
spends all her time in the kitchen. There's something in
the kitchen I have never seen before – a coffee grinder.
I never see any coffee beans – or tea leaves come to that.
They are kept under lock and key, like the Master's wine.
Your loving sister
Polly

Inside the houses

Regency Square's houses vary, not just in the number of storeys, but also in the dimensions of the building plots: some houses are wider and deeper than others. Even so, the internal layouts followed the same broad pattern, with the smartest rooms on the ground, first and second floors. The rooms became ever more modest, in size and fittings, higher up the house:

Attic: one, two or three bedrooms

Third floor: three or four bedrooms

Second floor: front best bedroom, back best bedroom

First floor: front drawing room, back drawing room

Ground floor: dining room and back room

Basement: housekeeper's room, kitchen, scullery

In some houses, the ground floor rooms were linked by folding doors.

There were no bathrooms, but the houses were built with an indoor toilet. This was variously on a half landing between the ground and first floors, or in a ground floor extension. The indoor toilets were fitted with mahogany seats and shelves. It's likely that the occupants of Regency Square's houses also had chamber pots in their bedrooms. A second toilet, in the yard, was for the servants.

Apart from the attic rooms, all rooms on the ground floor and upper storeys were fitted with bell pulls for summoning servants. The bell pulls were connected by wires to rows of bells in the basement passage.

Kitchens and sculleries

Kitchens and sculleries were in the basements. Basements had separate entrances and were formed from the foundations of the houses. It was common practice, when digging foundations, to deposit the excavated earth at the front and back of the house. The lower rooms became basements because the ground level was built up around them, leaving a narrow *area* for steps to the basement entrance.

Early inventories describe a complicated array of kitchen equipment: a cooking range with a spit rack, iron crane, and weights and pulleys for lifting; separate broiling and stewing stoves; dressers, cupboards and shelves; a copper boiler with its own furnace.

Sculleries had stone sinks, with water supplied through a tap or pump. No. 65 had a separate wash house with copper boiler, as well as a scullery.

In addition to the cupboards and dressers in the kitchen, basements had separate larders with shelves and iron meat hooks. Some houses also had a butler's pantry, with a sink and water supply, and a knife store. No. 20 had a wine cellar.

In 1827, the cook in charge of the kitchen at No. 15 was paid £10 a year, rising to £11 in 1830, equivalent to around £700 in today's money.

Water

There was no piped water supply at all in Brighton before 1834 and no widespread or reliable piped supply until the 1850s. Instead, water was drawn directly from wells. In the old town, there were some communal wells. In the new developments beyond the old town, wells were dug to supply individual premises or groups of neighbouring premises.

The houses in Regency Square had wells in the back yards, either for a single household's use or shared between neighbours. Water was either pumped directly from the well to the scullery sink, or to a cistern linked by lead pipe to the scullery sink tap. At least some houses had a force pump. These used

The east side of Regency Square, c. 1870s. No. 58, the second most valuable property in the square, is in the middle of the east side.
Courtesy of Chris Horlock.

a system of valves and pistons to pump water to a greater height, including to a cistern for the wc. Such houses therefore had a flushing indoor toilet.[19]

Heat, light and other comforts

The houses were heated with coal. This was delivered to coal cellars under the pavements. Some cast iron coal hole covers can still be seen in the pavements around the square.

---

19 Flushing toilets had been invented in the 18th century, although the flushing mechanism varied in design.

Coal was carried from the cellars in buckets and scuttles, through the basement and up the stairs to each room. Most rooms, even those in the attics, had fireplaces. The reception rooms and best bedrooms had elaborate fireplaces, with mantelpieces in black or white marble. Fire grates were decorated with brass or bronzed bars, and fluted and patterned iron work.

Register stoves are frequently mentioned in early inventories. These, too, were ornately decorated, sometimes with *japanning* (imitation lacquer work). Register stoves were a new invention, designed to regulate the draught, or air current, into the flue and radiate heat into the room. They consisted of an open fire grate set into an iron unit that filled the entire fireplace, effectively lining the fireplace in iron. Above the grate, at the entrance to the chimney, a moveable plate was raised or lowered to regulate the draught, or closed completely when the fire was not lit.

In rooms of lesser importance, mantelpieces were in wood and the fireplaces of much more basic design.

Regency Square was built just as Brighton acquired a gas works. From the mid-1820s, Brighton's street lighting was fuelled by coal gas, paid for as part of the town rates. But it is likely that Regency Square's early householders used candles and oil lamps to illuminate the interiors. Early inventories mention lamp brackets and lamp hooks in the halls and passages.

These inventories give clues to other fixtures and fittings in Regency Square houses: shelves, cupboards, stair rails and hat hooks in mahogany; brass door plates; brass eyes for stair carpets; rolling window blinds and sliding window shutters. The inventory for No. 20 itemised the front door bell *sunk in marble* and brass door numbers.

No. 5: Canoodling in the parlour

Throughout the 19th century and most of the 20th, one of the few grounds for ending a marriage was evidence of adultery *in flagrante delicto*. A husband seeking a legal separation might hire a private detective to witness him in the act of adultery. Naturally the gentleman could not possibly ask his mistress to subject herself to such a demeaning process. Young actresses were hired to play the role and be found with the guilty husband. It did not happen this way in 1839, when it was the wife who was deemed to be the guilty party. She was accused of *criminal conversation,* that is, committing adultery.

In 1837, Mrs Maria Therese Grant had fallen in love with Captain Arthur Vincent. She was the wife of Captain Alexander Grant; Arthur Vincent was captain of the ship carrying the Grant family homewards from Macao.

The Grants and their children landed at the Chain Pier in Brighton. They stayed briefly at the Norfolk Hotel before moving into a rented house at 5 Regency Square. Almost as soon as Captain Grant had absented himself by going to London, Captain Vincent visited Mrs Grant at home.

What was the proof of unacceptable behaviour by the couple? When Captain Grant finally sought a separation in 1839, the court heard that the couple had spent time alone on the ship and that they had been *observed sitting close to, and in earnest conversation with each other, and appeared much embarrassed and confused on finding that they were so observed; … on other occasions, Captain Vincent was seen kissing and taking personal liberties with Mrs Grant.*

Mrs Grant had allowed Captain Vincent to stay overnight at 5 Regency Square. The servants testified that *the parties were for the most part alone together, either in that room, or in the back drawing-room adjoining thereto, and communicating therewith by folding doors, into which back drawing-room a sofa, which usually stood in the front drawing-room, was removed by Mrs Grant's orders.*

The footman testified to *Captain Vincent's arm being round the waist of Mrs Grant* and that *Captain Vincent dined at the house that day, spent the evening and slept there, and for the purpose of his so doing, Mrs Grant hired a French bed for the night, and had it put up in the dressing-room of Captain Grant, which was below stairs.*

Later, Mrs Grant had requested that the cost of hiring the bed not be shown in her household accounts. Did she not wish her husband to think her spendthrift, or did she not want him to know of Captain Vincent's overnight stay?

So far, according to the judge, this was no evidence of adultery. All the maids declared that their mistress had at no time behaved improperly.

Imprudently, Mrs Grant had written four increasingly emotional letters to Captain Vincent, dated January 1838, from 5 Regency Square. The first letter is very long, verbose and in a mixture of English and French. It reads like a bad romantic novel: *Those only who have suffered them can tell the unhappy moments of separation … Now, I consider myself, in the silence of this night, lonely as the solitary dove, of which our love is the emblem in the fidelity of our hearts, inflamed with a delicious sentiment.*

There may be many excuses for this style of language. Mrs Grant had had many servants in China and, like any respectable captain's wife, she would have had time to read – mainly light novels, it can be surmised. English was possibly not her first language as she was a Creole from Mauritius, a French colony until 1810. Mrs Grant was therefore of French nationality when she was born. She was probably stunningly beautiful – but perhaps had had only the basic education allowed to women of her era.

The second of the four letters, much of it in French, borders on the hysterical and ends:

Adieu my dearest Arthur—I sincerely hope to hear something soon from you—I am so wretched that I am sure God will have pity on your poor and devoted Fri (torn off with the seal)
Believe me
Yours ever most affectt*
M. G.
Pray do kindly excuse my handwriting but I am so nervous that I cannot do anything well, it is a madness adieu

Mrs Grant seems to have been rather highly-strung. But how had these letters come into the possession of her husband? The lady had sent her letters to Captain Vincent care of the Jerusalem Coffee House in Cornhill, London. It would seem foolhardy for Mrs Grant to have used such a public place to send her letters, but this was where Captain Vincent might have done much of his business as the Jerusalem was described in 1866 as *one of the oldest of the City news-rooms, and is frequented by merchants and captains connected with the commerce of China, India, and Australia.* What she had forgotten was that her husband, also a sea captain, frequented the same coffee house.

Captain Grant spotted the letters in Captain Vincent's pigeon hole and, recognising his wife's writing, had seen fit to open them. Captain Grant immediately returned to Brighton with his friend Mr Bolton and his solicitor. His first action was to *search amongst her boxes for any letters which might have been addressed to her by Captain Vincent.* No letters from Captain Vincent were found. During the search, Mrs Grant was kept under surveillance in the drawing room by Mr Bolton. Such was a man's rights over his wife's life throughout the whole of the 19th century.

Mrs Grant was found guilty of criminal conversation. The judge was not unaware of how this would affect the family. Not only would Mrs Grant lose custody of her children but, as the judge stated in his summing up: *I find myself under the necessity,—notwithstanding all the difficulty and reluctance I feel to pronounce a sentence which shall consign this lady to infamy, and separate her from her husband and her family—of saying, that my mind is made up, that this lady has actually committed the offence imputed to her.*

Sewers and cess pits

Joshua Flesher Hanson built a sewer under the roads in front of the Regency Square houses. It was 6ft below the surface, 3ft high and 2ft wide, and ran down to the beach. It was completed by July 1820.

Householders were not allowed to put *privy soil or offensive matter* (in other words, waste from the toilets) into the sewer. In common with other sewers of the period, it was intended only as a rainwater drain. Across all of Brighton, it was illegal to use sewers for draining away foul water.

Regency Square houses were built with cess pits (or cesspools) in the back yards. Cess pits were periodically emptied by night soil men and *scavengers,* firms contracted by the town commissioners to remove *dust, dirt, filth, cinders and ashes* from houses in the town.

In reality, many households throughout the town disobeyed the law about discharging their privy soil into sewers. The residents of Regency Square were no exception: in 1826, residents complained that *night soil from privies* was running into the square's drains. Two years later, unable to cope with the quantity of waste, the Regency Square sewer overflowed.

Using rainwater sewers for household waste caused serious health concerns and, since the sewers drained onto the beaches, an unpleasant stink and pools of raw sewage along the shore. In 1833, the Brighton Guardian appealed to the town commissioners to *get rid of those nasty cesspools which at present disgrace our beach by reason of their forming large ponds at once both disgusting to the sight and the nostrils of the visitor.*

Back yard cess pits were no less a health hazard: they were often dug within a few feet of the household well. In 1830, the town commissioners investigated a complaint by the occupant of No. 7 Regency Square and discovered that the contents of cess pits belonging to two houses in Preston Street were soaking through the wall into No. 7's kitchen.

All-purpose sewers, as we understand the word today, were not constructed in Brighton until the 1870s. In Regency Square, the new sewers ran along the front of the houses on the north side of the square, but behind the houses on the east and west sides, running down Preston Street and Queensbury Mews.

Although the town paid for the new sewers to be laid, householders had to make their own arrangements for connecting to them. In Regency Square, this meant paying for back yards to be dug up and drains laid. In houses on the north side of the square, basement floors had to be dug up, so that drains could be laid from the backs of the houses to the new sewer at the front.

Some householders in Regency Square engaged builders to carry out the work as soon as the new sewers were in place: the owner of No. 61 had plans drawn up in June 1872. These specify a 6in drain to connect with the main sewer in Queensbury Mews and the *cesspool to be emptied and filled up solid with earth and chalk*. Most householders in Regency Square did not arrange for a connection to the new sewers till the 1890s. They may have delayed because of the expense and upheaval, or simply because local builders could not keep pace with demand. In all cases, the work involved emptying and filling in the household's cess pit, sometimes with a domed brick cap, as well as laying a new drain.

There are nearly eight thousand houses at present in the parish, all of which excepting smaller tenements obtain their supply of water from wells on the premises, many of which during the last summer were dry for a considerable period. The houses in Brighton having no drains which communicate with any channel to take away waste water, are of necessity obliged to have Cess-pools into which it is conveyed, and from thence in many instances it has percolated adjacent wells.

Extract from an advertisement by The Brighton Water Company, Brighton Gazette, 19 January 1826

The central gardens

An exclusive space

Under the Regency Square covenants, the central gardens were for the exclusive use of *privileged* householders (that is, all except those at Nos. 44 to 50, in the north-east corner of the square). Privileged householders were required to pay towards the upkeep of the lawn and its railings, in return for which they were issued with a key to a gate.

The covenants were to last until 1889, but in 1885, under the powers of the Brighton Improvement Act 1884, Brighton Corporation compulsorily purchased the garden. The corporation paid only £50 for it, which seems a very small sum compared to the price that Joshua Flesher Hanson had paid for the land in 1818. Hanson's heirs contested the corporation's offer and the matter went to an inquiry, held before a jury and the Sheriff of Sussex, at the Old Ship in April 1885. The jury ruled in the corporation's favour.

The gardens nonetheless remained accessible only to Regency Square residents until WW2.

A car park

On 19 January 1963, the Brighton Evening Argus published a 3-column photograph of *Brighton's picturesque Regency Square* under the heading:

CAR PARK PLAN FOR REGENCY
SQUARE LAWNS

According to the newspaper, the borough council's Watch Committee had proposed erecting *a rented lock up car park for residents who in March will have parking meters outside their homes*. The rest of the lawns would be turned over to a car park for the general public. Conscious that there might be objections to such a plan, the committee was quick to state that *it is the committee's intention to make the car park as attractive as possible … Potted shrubs and plants would be laid out to retain a green atmosphere*.

There was a suggestion that a car park be put under the square, but that was out of the question as the cost would be *astronomical*.

The 1963 plan was not put into action. Conservationists (and perhaps even some car-owning residents) heaved a sigh of relief. But it was to be a short-lived relief. The *astronomical* amount of money was found.

Regency Square's lawn in 1967, immediately before the
underground car park was constructed.
Courtesy of Chris Horlock.

A proposed design for the lawns of Regency Square c.1966
Courtesy of the Regency Society

The Regency Society of Brighton and Hove, which had been founded in 1945 to protect the towns' historic heritage, set about trying to mitigate the disaster. In 1966, architect John Leopold Denman was in the last year of his 14-year stint as Regency Society chairman. Under Denman's chairmanship, the society produced a design for the reconstruction of the gardens. The design was drawn up either by Denman himself or within his architectural practice of Denman and Son.

On the back of the design pictured above, the Regency Society advised:

Should the Brighton Borough Council decide to form the underground car park in the central area of this Square, the Regency Society of Brighton and Hove strongly advocates that it should be covered by a formal garden in harmony with this dignified square, with the provision of sheltered seats, flower beds, lawns and trees as indicated by the accompanying drawing. If the floor level of the car park is raised and covered with terraced roofing, as shown (in the proposal), the saving in cost on the excavation will be adequate to provide a garden of this description.

Work started on the underground car park in 1967. The Regency Society's design was largely implemented, although not adhered to in all its details. Some of the structures on the south garden would have been costly to build and maintain, and there is not a sufficient depth of soil to plant trees. From 1967 until a major refurbishment in 2003, the car park had public toilets and even a tiny underground police office.

The Regency Society's design for the gardens is now so familiar that residents and business owners have said they do not want the basic layout to be altered. But, at the time of writing in 2018, the gardens are beginning to look ragged and uncared for – a result of public purse tightening. The Regency Square Regeneration Partnership hopes to receive funding, through an agreement between Brighton & Hove City Council and British Airways i360, to renovate the gardens.

No. 18: From disaster to success

No. 18 Regency Square was completed by 1822. For the next 20 years, the Brighton Gazette's *Fashionable Chronicle* column reported a constant stream of arrivals and departures at the house, a sure sign that it was a lodging house.

In 1842, the house was sold to a widow, Mrs Cloves. At 10.38 on the morning of 1 November 1852, the train in which Mrs Cloves was travelling to London hurtled into a goods train at Redhill station. Mrs Cloves was seriously injured with multiple fractures to her leg. Other passengers on the train, including the Earl of Chichester, Mr and Mrs Tamplin of the brewing family, and Mrs Dives of 16 Regency Square suffered minor injuries.

Mrs Cloves was brought home to Regency Square, where she died on 21 November. At the inquest, held at the Royal Sovereign in Preston Street, the verdict was not that Mrs Cloves had died of her injuries, but that she had *died from fatty degeneration of the heart of long standing*. No compensation for Mrs Cloves' family, then. However, three 'servants' of the railway company were sentenced to two months' imprisonment with hard labour for causing the collision by a violation of the company's orders.

No. 18 then became the possession of Dr James William Wilson and his wife, Maria. Forty years later Mrs Wilson sold the house, which briefly reverted to its original use as a lodging house before coming into the ownership of the Stoner family. By 1895, John Nathan Stoner and his 22-year old son Harold Boniface Stoner were running a dental practice from the property. Stoner senior retired around 1908 and, by 1911, Harold and his wife were living at the house.

Harold's younger brother, Patrick Stoner, was also a dentist and joined the practice at No. 18. Patrick threw himself into his work and social activities.

In 1930/31 he was the President of the Southern Branch of the British Dental Association after serving for several years as its Secretary. He served an almost unbroken stint as a member of the Regency Square Management Committee from 1930 until a few months before his death in April 1944. His wife, Dorothy, was a pianist *whose lightness of touch never fails to arouse admiration* at concerts around Sussex.

Patrick and Dorothy had a daughter, Priscilla, who inherited her mother's musical talent. As a teenager, she too was playing locally, occasionally with the talented Brighton College violinist, John Atkin Swan. In September 1943, they announced their engagement and in the following September they were married.

The marriage was short-lived. In the early 1950s, Scylla, as she became known professionally, married cellist John Kennedy. Their son, violinist Nigel Kennedy, was born in Brighton in 1956 and spent some of his early years at 18 Regency Square, with his mother and maternal grandmother.

The house was a dentist's surgery again when Roy Gilles had his practice at No. 18 in the early 1960s. But by 1966 the property belonged to former band-leader Alf Feld. Mr Feld was locally famous as the owner of a succession of Brighton hotels (Regency Square's Beach Hotel, the Norfolk Hotel in Kings Road and the Resort Hotel in Preston Road) and as Mayor of Brighton in 1979.

No. 18 has more recently been the Dove Hotel and part of Topps Hotel, and is now private apartments.

The Mews

Regency Mews

Initially known as Upper Regency Mews or North Regency Mews, to distinguish it from Lower Regency Mews (now Queensbury Mews), this mews did not serve the normal function of providing private stabling attached to the large houses in the square. This is because the land rises behind Regency Square and the back yards of the houses in the north terrace are often as much as 10ft below the ground level of the mews. This mews was therefore used for livery stables.

Construction of Upper Regency Mews began shortly after 1822, but Hanson neglected to install a drain in the road. Householders on the north side of Regency Square complained to the town commissioners that water from the mews ran into their properties. At first, the commissioners replied that it was not their problem, but in 1827 they instructed that a *proper drainage channel* must be installed.

There were three entrances to Regency Mews: one from Preston Street and a second from Russell Square, both still existing. The third was via the carriage entrance at 43 Regency Square.

One of the livery stables belonged first to Mr West and then passed into the hands of Mr Silverthorne. Another was run by Mr Nye.

By the end of the 19th century, horses had been replaced in the mews by first a bicycle dealership and finally by Moore's Garage. Ironically, there was a moment in the history of the garage which harked back very much to a previous era:

There are tales of the garage having serviced military tanks during WW2. Given the narrowness of the entrances to the garage, this seems unlikely, but there is no doubt that it was very active during that time as an emergency fire station and servicing home guard vehicles. After the war, Moore's Garage specialised in a rather better class of vehicle (Daimler and Jaguar, amongst others) and had showrooms elsewhere in the town.

Moore's Garage was at the eastern end of Regency Mews, the section now known as Russell Mews. In the early 1980s the whole of this end of Regency Mews was sold off for redevelopment. In place of the garage rose the five-storey Russell House (originally offices, now converted into 50 flats and studio apartments) and a small gated community of 15 houses and flats.

The western end of the mews retains the name Regency Mews and, on its north side, still shows traces of its original function as livery stabling and coach houses.

Queensbury Mews

Queensbury Mews was constructed from 1823. It started life as stables and coach-houses serving Nos. 51 to 66 Regency Square as well as 123–130 Kings Road. There was accommodation above for the coachmen and their families.

It was known as Lower Regency Mews until the 1840s and, as late as 1860, there was still some doubt about the name of the street – as the little tiff over who paid rates on which property shows. For the sake of convenience, let's call it by its modern name.

As with Regency Mews, Hanson neglected to install a drain in Queensbury
Mews. Owners of Kings Road houses at the bottom of the mews complained
that water from Queensbury Mews ran into the backs of their properties. At
the end of 1828, the town commissioners demanded that Queensbury Mews
be properly finished, with pavements and water channels on either side of a
carriage road.

Queensbury Mews had one grand building. St Margaret's Church in St
Margaret's Place had been built in 1824. Its imposing west wall, containing a

*The west façade of St
Margaret's Church. The
garage to the left of the
church was converted to a
house, 51a Regency Square,
in the 21st century.*

*James Gray Collection,
Courtesy of the Regency
Society*

massive rose window, as well as its back door, dominated the upper end of the mews.

In 1837, the Edmund Clay Memorial School opened for children aged 5 to *not very old*, there being no compulsory schooling at that time.

As early as 1839, there was a beer seller at the back of 123 Kings Road. For many years in the 20th century, this public house was affectionately known as The Hole in the Wall. Today it is better known by its official title: The Queensbury Arms.

In the 1860s and 1870s, Mr Beck of 123 Kings Road also owned a ramshackle property opposite his tiny ale house in Queensbury Mews. In the early 1880s he sold the site to the congregation of the French Protestant Church who had been priced out of their place of worship in St Margaret's Place.

The Edmund Clay Memorial School immediately prior to its demolition in 1962. To the left of the school is the space left by the demolition of St Margaret's Church. The site of the church and school is now occupied by the exhibition hall of the Hilton Brighton Metropole.

James Gray Collection, Courtesy of the Regency Society

On 18 July 1887, the little red brick church was officially opened for services. It still stands today, but it is now a private home.

As time passed, Queensbury Mews premises changed from private stables to cab or fly stables (usually small family businesses with the owner and family living above the shop), cheap housing and services for motor vehicles. At the beginning of the 20th century, No. 1 Queensbury Mews switched from one type of horse-power to the other when Henry Morley opened his FIAT Motor Garage. By 1921, Miss Martyn had taken over the premises for her taxi firm, advertising *smart landaulettes and touring cars for hire*. Cars continued to dominate the southern end of the mews until the late 1990s when No. 1 was redeveloped to become a private house.

Nos. 1 and 2 are all that remains of the original stabling in Queensbury Mews. Nos. 3 to 15 are late 20th century additions to the street.

No. 45: Shots and screams

It is 2.50pm on 20 September 1931: a quiet Sunday afternoon in Regency Square. It has been a busy week in the boarding house at No. 45 but for just for a few hours, Isabella Hargreaves and her companion, 16-year-old Hilda Lawford, are resting in the basement. The doorbell rings. Hilda is sent upstairs to find out who it is.

Hilda opens the door and screams. Before her stands Harry Cashford. In his left hand he holds a pistol. Seconds later, Harry has fired a shot into Hilda's face. Luckily, he shoots wide, merely grazing her cheek and breaking a fanlight above the inner door behind her. Hilda knows, moreover, that it is Isabella who is Harry's real target. He pushes past Hilda towards Isabella, standing at the top of the basement stairs. Isabella turns and manages to reach the bottom of the basement stairs before she hears the second shot. Harry Cashford has fired a single bullet from his *six-chambered Webley Service Revolver* into his brain. At 4.16 the same day, at the Royal Sussex County Hospital, he is pronounced dead.

What provoked this violent attack and why did Harry Cashford commit suicide? Harry and Isabella had previously lived as man and wife for some six years, arriving at 45 Regency Square in December 1930. Harry's behaviour, however, had since become rather erratic. In January, he had brought a girlfriend into the house, at which point, understandably, Isabella refused to continue to live with him. He became threatening; so much so that Isabella applied to the Police Court for protection from him. In August, he moved out of Regency Square, but not far away. He took a room at 6 Sillwood Street, from where there was a short cut to Regency Square through a twitten between Little Preston Street and Preston Street. Isabella gave him £15 to stay away, but still the threat continued.

Was Harry vindictive or insane? When Police Sergeant Wren, the Coroner's Officer, searched Harry's room in Sillwood Street that night he found a 14-page document dated the previous day. At the Inquest, the Coroner refused to read parts of the document, deeming them an *absolute abuse of certain well-known people living in the town*. This might lead us to think that Harry was paranoid or suffered from delusions. The parts that the Coroner did read out made sad listening: *If I fail it means hanging or imprisonment for life and I don't want to linger on. You can give my rotten body to any hospital who cares to accept it. I hope to injure her and not to kill her so she will have to face up to the world after what is about to happen.*

It is worth reflecting that, had Harry lived, he would have been punished not only for attempted murder, he would also have been found guilty of the heinous crime of attempted suicide; punishable, until 1961, by imprisonment.

The Coroner further expurgated the text, jumping to a later part of Harry's document: *If I am successful tomorrow and can fix things I shall be happy. At present I am lonely. Any good things I have got on at different places, they may keep themselves as I won't need the money after tomorrow, Sunday. I am just going round to 45 Regency Square. I sincerely hope I find someone there. This is the Journey's end. I can't stand it any longer.*

Harry Cashford might well have been mad and bad, but today, reading his last testament, he also appears to be a victim of severe depression. At the end of the Inquest the Coroner, in measured tones, pronounced his verdict: *In this case, of course, I must find that the man committed suicide whilst of unsound mind.*

The Seafront

Nowadays, Brighton's seafront is a major thoroughfare for pedestrians and vehicles, but until the 1820s it was an unreliable route. It was sometimes closed to carriages travelling west beyond Middle Street. In 1821, various townsmen contributed to the cost of making the seafront road fit for carriages as far as West Street.[20] George IV opened the new road, called *King's Road*, in 1822.

Two years later, some of the residents of Bedford Square clubbed together to create a walk, 6ft wide, along the seafront between Montpelier Road and the newly erected Norfolk Hotel. According to the Brighton Guardian, the seafront near Bedford Square had, until then, been in *a useless and disreputable state*. It was not unknown for the seafront and beach west of the old town to be used for fly-tipping building waste. The new seafront walk permitted residents to *promenade, uninterrupted by the turmoil and bustle, not to mention the other nuisances met with on the pavé*.

James Robison, a resident of Regency Square, thought Bedford Square's seafront walk such a good idea that he proposed extending and expanding it, to create an esplanade. Support was not immediately forthcoming and it was 1827 before Robison could begin the work. He arranged for the cliff top to be made more level between Cannon Place and Preston Street, for steps to the beach to be constructed near Regency Square, and the cliff embankment to be turfed and protected by large sandstones.

---

20 This seems at odds with Baxter's 1822 directory, which recommended excursions from Brighton to Worthing *along the cliff*. The seafront villas built west of the old town in the early 1800s must also have been accessible by horse drawn vehicles. Perhaps the seafront route was viable for carriages only in certain weathers or seasons, but adequate for people on horseback or on foot. Sedan chairs were also available for the well-to-do. In 1810, a sedan chair from the town centre to Belle Vue cost 2s 6d (roughly £5.80 in today's money).

Robison's esplanade idea was taken up along other parts of the seafront, including by the developers of Brunswick Square. By the early 1830s, the town commissioners had taken over the project, widening the new esplanades and the road itself.

Royal Sussex Regiment Memorial

> The Mayor (Alderman J. C. Buckwell) and Corporation of Brighton have offered a site at the south end of Regency Square, facing the West Pier for the erection of a memorial to the officers, non-commissioned officers, and men of the Royal Sussex Regiment who fell in the South African War.
>
> *Brighton Gazette 5 March 1903*

Although the Regency Square Management Committee of the day does not seem to have been consulted on whether a memorial to the fallen of the Boer war should be erected in the square, it is clear that they approved. When Colonel Cecil Somers Clarke, grandson of the doughty Somers Clarke,[21] asked the committee for *permission for the friends of the various officers of the Battalions who would be invited to attend at the unveiling of the South African Memorial on the 29 October 1904 to go into the enclosed grounds of the Square and for the Band of the 1st Volunteer Battalion of the Royal Sussex Regiment to play at such unveiling* it was granted unanimously.

The dignitaries attending the opening ceremony, including two dukes, one lord, one bishop and numerous colonels, were led by the Marquess of Abergavenny in his role as Lord Lieutenant of Sussex. Alas, the main body of the very regiment which the monument honours was abroad on active service. However, they were represented by the Volunteers *who lent colour and dignity to the proceedings.*

---

21 We meet Somers Clarke later. He was a leading light in Regency Square's management committee in the 19th century.

Colonel Donne, standing in for Sir William Kell, *the gallant officer at the head of the regiment,* explained to the gathered crowd that:

> *The statue which surmounted the pedestal took its origin from an incident at the battle of Doornkop, in which the regiment took a conspicuous part … it was the sergeant bugler of the Royal Sussex Regiment who sounded the charge to the troops on that day, with the result that the whole brigade charged and soon swept the Boers from their formidable position.*

In his speech, Colonel Donne mentions the sculptor, Charles Hartwell. It is generally believed today that Hartwell's model for the statue of the bugler was Sergeant Tom Gates, who had served with the Royal Sussex Regiment in South Africa. The memorial was constructed by the firm of B&W Bennett, based in Lewes Road.

In more recent years, the dates of the First and Second World Wars have been added to the memorial. A wreath is laid at a ceremony on 11 November each year.

Unveiling ceremony of the Royal Sussex Regiment memorial, 29 October 1904 (source unknown)

The West Pier

Today, the most visible feature on the seafront opposite Regency Square is the British Airways i360. From the mid-1860s, until construction of the i360 in 2014, the most visible seafront feature was the West Pier.

The West Pier was designed by Eugenius Birch. Construction began in 1863 and the pier opened in 1866. Extending for more than 1,000 feet over the beach and sea, the pier was designed for promenading. A well-known and rather imperious resident of Regency Square, Mr Somers Clarke, objected strongly to the large size of the pier's toll booths. There is little evidence that his objections met with much support locally.

Towards the end of the 19th century, a pavilion (later converted to a theatre) and a landing stage for vessels were added to the seaward end. A concert hall was added to the middle of the pier in 1916.

The pier closed, in poor repair, in 1975. The West Pier Trust, established in 1978, campaigned for the pier to be saved and restored, but storms and fire hastened its collapse into the sea.

The New Pier, Brighton 1866
Courtesy of Royal Pavilion & Museums, Brighton & Hove

No. 21: A house of many talents

Edward Sutton and his family live in Brighton. In addition to being a chemist, he is public analyst for the County of Sussex. In his official work he is a slave to duty. In his relationship towards his family he is also ruled by what he considers to be his duty. He refuses to let his daughter pursue a singing career and reproves his son for corresponding with a girl with whom he is adolescently in love. His gentle wife gently remonstrates with him for this, warning him that by constant repression he will lose his children's trust and confidence – but he insists that his method is right, not realising what is about to happen to certain members of his family.

Eastbourne Herald 25 May 1946

Part of an advertisement for the film, based on the play,
'Pink String and Sealing Wax'

The popular play *Pink String and Sealing Wax* was first staged at the Theatre Royal in Brighton on 9 August 1943. A little escapism at a terrible time. The play was turned into a film in 1945. But the connection with Regency Square?

In January 1829, a young chemist named Richard Coley Moore opened his very first shop at 44 Preston Street. By 1831, Richard's business was doing well. He was employing assistant chemists, one of whom was a certain Edward Heath.

1832 saw Richard Moore and Edward Heath involved in a manslaughter case. Heath had made up an urgent prescription for Captain Burdett, who lived in Western Road. The prescription was for:

1½ oz of infusion of senna

2 drachms of tincture of senna

4 drachms or ½ oz of Epsom salts.

Poor Captain Burdett was suffering no more than constipation. Alas, Heath had made a fatal mistake. He had included oil of tar in the concoction. It killed the Captain. Richard Moore immediately dismissed Heath, who disappeared. At the Coroner's inquest, in May 1832, Heath was charged in his absence with manslaughter and a warrant issued for his arrest.

Richard Moore's business was clearly not affected by the scandal as it continued to prosper. During the 1830s, he not only practised as a dispensing chemist, he was also, ironically, an agent for the Universal Life Insurance Company.

By 1841, the shop was at 67 Preston Street. No. 67 Preston Street is at the corner of Regency Square and part of the same building as 21 Regency Square.

Richard Moore died in 1867, having already passed the business on to his eldest son Edward. The name of the enterprise had evolved from R. MOORE, CHEMIST to R MOORE AND SON, CHEMISTS AND MINERAL WATER MANUFACTURERS.

Like his father, Edward was more than a dispensing chemist: he was also the Town Analyst. As Town Analyst he perhaps felt that an address in Preston Street did not reflect his status. By 1870 he had moved his family into the adjoining 21 Regency Square.

GAS METER TESTING HOUSE

The Gas Committee's proceedings contained the following:

RESOLVED -That Mr Edward Moore, of Preston Street, Brighton, be appointed to examine the apparatus in the gas meter testing house, and to make from time to time, when requested by the committee, the necessary tests of the illuminating power and purity of the gas under the 41st section of the 'Brighton and Hove General Gas Company's Act, 1866'.

Brighton Gazette 10 December 1867

Edward and his wife Emily produced 10 children: Emily, Henry, Ada, Bertha, Jessie, Edith, Ida, Eva, Mabel and Lilian. Edith did not survive infancy, but almost all of the other nine children became successful in their own sphere of life.

Henry set up business at 68 Preston Street as an agent for the new-fangled Humber bicycle. He later became the owner of MOORE'S MOTOR GARAGE, which expanded to fill much of the eastern end of Regency Mews.

Emily, Ada, Bertha, Jessie, Ida and Lilian became professional singers.

Four of Edward Moore's daughters, all of whom grew up at 21 Regency Square /
67 Preston Street
© National Portrait Gallery, London

As the tenth child in the family, Lilian's middle name was Decima – the name she used professionally. In 1896, at the age of only 17, Decima was recruited into the D'Oyly Carte Opera Company to sing the role of Casilda in the Gilbert and Sullivan opera *The Gondoliers*.

In 1905, after a successful career in plays, musicals, concerts and light opera, Decima married Brigadier-General Sir Frederick Gordon Guggisberg. Sir Frederick had a distinguished career in West Africa and in 1919 was appointed Governor General of the Gold Coast. Decima's obituary in 1964 reveals that she played a very active part in public service in her own right.

In 1912, Ada and Decima had marched together under the banner of the Actresses' Franchise League, part of the campaign for women's right to vote in England. Ada also campaigned internationally, attending the 1920 International Women's Suffrage Alliance Congress in Geneva.

Eva was a professional dancer and actress. It is claimed that she taught Winston Churchill to dance at his prep school in Brunswick Road and that she thought him *the naughtiest small boy in the world*. She appeared in plays and eventually became a well-known character actress in the cinema, appearing in over 30 films between 1920 and 1946, including *The Old Dark House*, with Charles Laughton.

Eva Moore in the 'The Old Dark House" (Universal Pictures, 1932) with Charles Laughton (Wikimedia Commons: public domain)

Eva's son, Jack Esmond, became a theatrical producer and actor. Her daughter, Jill Esmond, became the first Mrs Laurence Olivier and a well-respected actress. Bertha's son also had a stage and cinema career.

On 3 April 1882, Emily married Charles Pertwee at St Peter's Church in Brighton. They had two sons, Ernest and Roland.

Roland Pertwee was in turn father to Michael (born 1916) and John Devon (born 1919). Michael is credited, alongside his father, with having written the first British soap opera for television, *The Grove Family* (1954–1957). John Devon Pertwee is better known today as Jon Pertwee, who played Dr Who and Worzel Gummidge.

And the author of *Pink String and Sealing Wax*? None other than Roland Pertwee, grandson of the Town Analyst of Brighton.

Regency Square's management committees

1818–1884

Joshua Flesher Hanson drew up detailed covenants, to remain in force until Christmas Day 1889, to ensure that the appearance of the square was preserved. The covenants included a requirement for *privileged* householders – those enjoying access to the central garden – to pay a share of the costs of maintaining the lawn, the roads around the square and the sewer. The amount that householders paid was to be set by a committee, who would also decide what colour the railings and external woodwork of the houses should be repainted.

Aside from Hanson himself, the committee was to consist of four owners or occupiers of houses in the square, elected by all other householders. One of the earliest committee members was probably James Robison, who had bought No. 15 Regency Square in 1821. Robison wrote to the town commissioners several times in the 1820s, drawing attention to problems, seemingly on behalf of other residents. However, there are no surviving records of the committee's activities in the first 50 years after the completion of the square.

By the late 1870s, it is probable that the committee consisted of the following men:

> Mr Cobbett Derby of 12 Regency Square
> Mr Tilson Humphrey Mosley of Rose Hill
> Mr James Martin Jnr of Elmsleigh
> Dr Richard Dell of 19 Regency Square
> Col J W Silverthorne JP of 43 Regency Square
> Mr Somers Clarke of 57 Regency Square.

Somers Clarke was a local solicitor, and clerk to the parish Vestry between 1830 and 1892. The Vestry was the body responsible for managing churches, cemeteries and the workhouse.

At the start of the 1880s, the Regency Square committee realised that the covenants were due to expire. Determined not to let the strict management of the square be weakened, they proposed, in January 1883, a Bill to Parliament. The Bill sought *powers to preserve and manage the lawn in the middle of the Square etc. the acquisition, by compulsion if necessary, and vesting of the same in the Mayor for the time being of Brighton; to perpetuate the covenants entered into the deeds …*

The Bill had no success but might well have inspired the borough council to use the proposed Brighton Improvement Bill of 1884, most of which was concerned with sanitation in the town, to acquire many of the central gardens in the town's squares. This move worried Somers Clarke, who could see power over Regency Square being taken away from him. In early 1884, he set about persuading the council to insert a provision for the continuation of the covenants in perpetuity.

Councillors were clearly aware of Mr Somers Clarke's reputation as somewhat of a lone wolf. Questions were asked:

> Mr STYER said he should like to ask the Town Clark how many owners of property in Regency Square had authorised Mr Somers Clarke to make this suggestion.
>
> The TOWN CLERK replied that he could not answer the questions, except by saying that he presumed Mr Clarke was acting for all; he was instructed by the Regency Square Committee of Management.
>
> Mr STYER said he was given to understand that there was a strong feeling among the owners of property in the square against the covenants referred to becoming perpetual. They dealt with such matters as the number and size of windows, elevation of the houses etc. and there was an objection to these covenants being continued after the expiration of the existing leases, which would be seven years hence. He did not think that the Council had anything to do with matters of that sort, and he was told that Mr Somers Clarke had made this suggestion individually.
>
> *Brighton Gazette, 2 February 1884*

In the end, the covenants were added to the Bill and the Brighton Improvement Act 1884 came into effect.

1885–1944

Somers Clarke immediately set up a successor to Hanson's committee. The nominal chair was, in perpetuity, the Mayor of Brighton. The first meeting was held on 4 September 1885 in Brighton Town Hall. Five committee members were elected, all nominated by Somers Clarke:

> Somers Clarke
> John Paling
> William Loton of 30 Regency Square
> Elisha Lewis of 32 Regency Square
> James Martin of Elmsleigh

The committee appointed, as its solicitors, Howlett and Clarke of Ship Street – the firm in which Somers Clarke was a partner.

Mr Somers Clarke (1802–1892)
served as Clerk to the Brighton Vestry
for over 60 years and was senior partner
in a well-known firm of solicitors in
Ship Street.

Courtesy of Royal Pavilion &
Museums, Brighton & Hove

Enthusiasm for setting up a committee seems to have been very limited among the square's other householders. Despite a *copy of the notice of the meeting left in each privileged house and a letter sent to last address of all known owners*, the only men present apart from those elected were the Mayor, Colonel William Silverthorne, a Mr Jones and a Mr Smith.

It was not until 1896 that the first woman was elected onto the committee: Miss Vincent, a boarding house keeper at No. 31.

Maintaining the lawn

The committee continued to levy a rate on Regency Square householders to pay for the upkeep of the lawn, its railings and lamps. Estate agents Jenner and Dell, whose offices were at 22 Regency Square, were employed as collecting agents. They frequently had to deal with late payment. Defaulters were threatened with legal action.

In 1885, the rate was 3*d* in the pound of the value of each house. It gradually increased to 4*d* by 1918, then jumped to 6*d* in 1919. This might well have been to enable the committee to repair the neglect of the lawn during WW1. The rate fluctuated over the next 20 years, but was back to 6*d* in 1940 *having regard to the painting having to be done next year.* Whether that painting was done is doubtful given WW2.

The rate funded the employment of a gardener and a constable. Each was paid 18/- per week in 1885. In 1894, the constable was found to be wanting and the committee had to remind him of his duties:

> *As the Constable does not seem to appear to have thoroughly understood his duties in connection with the Management of the Square, the Committee having such and considered the question have <u>Resolved</u> That the Constable devote the whole of the morning up to one o'clock in attending to the Enclosure and that he parade the Square in Livery in the afternoon.*
>
> *<u>Resolved</u> That the Constable be granted permission to carry luggage provided it be done with dispatch.*

Two years later, the constable was still not giving satisfaction. It looks as if he had been doing odd jobs locally on committee time. Once again, his duties were spelled out to him.

Rules for the constable – Extract

Attendance (Sundays excepted) shall be from the 1st October to 1st March from 9 am to sunset and from 2nd March to 30th September from 8 am to sunset.

If the Committee find the work in the Enclosure has not been neglected they will be willing to consider an application of the Constable for an occasional holiday.

If the Constable require assistance he may obtain the same at his own Expense provided always that the Constable is also in attendance.

The Constable shall until further notice be allowed to carry luggage to and from houses in this Square only, provided it does not interfere with his regular work.

No window cleaning or any other work except luggage as above during duty hours will be allowed.

The Constable shall discourage organ grinders whether blind or otherwise, tramps, beggar singers and other objectionable noises that disturb the quietude of the Square and under no circumstances are two sets of […][22] or singers with Pianos or other instruments to be allowed to play at the same time in the Square.

He kept his job until 1897, at which point he was *given the chance to resign before he is dismissed.* The gardener, Theodore Charles Harris, added the post of constable to his existing tasks.

The committee built a tool shed for gardener Harris in the enclosure; spent £5 per year on his clothing; paid for euonymus bushes and sycamore trees to plant; bought a roller and, after some agonising over the expense, a Shank's 19-inch lawnmower in 1891 (possibly not replaced until it was decided to buy a motor mower in 1927).

Mr Harris received his first pay rise, to £1 a week, in 1915. By 1917, he was beginning to feel somewhat underpaid. The committee agreed to add 4/- to his salary, in addition to his war bonus of 4/-, bringing his wage up to £1 8s. Mr Harris' plea that he needed £1 15s a week in order to be able to live went unheeded. A Minute of 1 May 1919 states that Robert Edward Hillier had replaced Mr Harris as new gardener – at the wage of £1 15s per week.

---

22 Here the committee used a racially offensive word.

Complaints

As wealthier residents began to desert the square, properties in Queensbury Mews were gradually given over to commercial fly stables. These caused complaints and the management committee had to ask the borough council's Watch Committee to address the problem.

> *The Management Committee of Regency Square having received from Owners and Occupiers of Houses in the Square repeated complaints of the great and increasing nuisance caused by the Cabs and Cabmen who stand (often to the number of 30 or 40) in the Queensbury Mews and whose noise, shouting and obscene language is most annoying to the visitors. The smell also in the Mews Road is most unpleasant and as the warm weather comes on the nuisance from this alone will be unbearable. The Regency Square Committee therefore on behalf of the Owners, Occupiers and Visitors most urgently request the Watch Committee to take prompt measures to remove the nuisance.*
>
> *Minute of 18 April 1891*

In 1924, motor vehicles were causing similar complaints.

> *… the nuisance to the inhabitants of the privileged houses in the Square caused by numerous motor vehicles being driven into the Square and left there unattended for several hours together and the unloading of passengers from Charabanc's [sic] and reloading the same later…*

Some residents complained about children. In May 1884 a letter was read to the borough Watch Committee *from Mr A. Mackintosh of 47 Regency Square complaining of the annoyance caused by the children attending St Margaret's Schools in Queensbury Mews.* At the committee's 1941 AGM, a rather radical solution was suggested in response to complaints about children trespassing on the lawn:

> *The Chairman Mr Holtorp would try to get more Police Supervision but he pointed out that the Enclosure was private ground and the police could only enter it at the request of one of the Committee. He would also see Messrs Jenner and Dell with regard to having the locks on the gates repaired so that the gates could be kept shut and also try to arrange for the fences to have barbed wire placed upon them in the hope that this would prevent children trespassing in the Enclosure.*

Then there was the vexed question of games. A lawn tennis club was founded in 1896, but other games were prohibited.

No person entitled to admission to the Enclosure shall at any time in the Enclosure play at cricket, rounders, football or any game of ball or other game likely to damage the trees, shrubs, flowerbeds or which may interfere with the full enjoyment of the Enclosure by all persons entitled thereto, provided this Bye-Law shall not be deemed to prohibit the game of tennis and croquet on such parts of the Enclosure as shall be allotted by the Committee therefor.

The penalty for playing cricket and other games on the lawn was £2.

The square remained under the control of its management committee until 1944 when, under Section 271(i) of the 1931 Brighton Corporation Act, the committee ceased to exist.

Following WW2, Regency Square was in a pitiful state. The lawn had lost its railings, the widespread shortage of housing meant that houses were divided into very small flatlets and rooms. It was even, for a brief spell, the red-light district of west Brighton. Nobody seemed to care for it any longer.

Regency Square had deteriorated considerably during WW2. Much of Brighton was photographed in 1945 for the National Building Register. Miss Ormerod took this photograph and several others of the square in 1946. Courtesy of Historic England

Regency Square Area Society, 1979 – 2018

The Regency Square Area Society was formed in March 1979. It developed out of a campaign to deal with the noise and disturbance from a late-night drinking club in the basement of the George IV Hotel (now George IV Mansions). Residents felt they had been let down by the licensing authority who had allowed such a club in an area of homes and quiet hotels. A group of residents organised a public meeting in the Portland House Hotel (now Hotel Una), formed the Regency Square Area Society, and elected its first committee and officers:

Chairman – Eddie Edwards, 38 Regency Square (retired engineer)
Secretary – Carol Clipsham, Adelaide Hotel, 51 Regency Square (hotelier)
Treasurer – Roger Hinton, 38 Regency Square (administrator)

The aims of the society are to:

- Pursue matters of common interest to those living and working in the Regency Square area
- Preserve and improve the character and environment of the area
- Encourage good neighbourliness
- Contribute as a local community to the life of the city

The RSAS committee has always monitored planning applications affecting the area. It campaigned to reduce the proposed height of Russell House, Russell Mews in 1988. The building would have loomed over the north terrace had the developers had their way. In 2001, the Save Our Seafront campaign, to prevent a three-storey building being built to the south of the promenade, was costly but influential.

Children's parties were among the great successes in the society's early years. Other social events brought the community together. There have been festivals on the lawn to celebrate Royal Weddings in 1981 and 1986, and the Queen's Golden Jubilee in 2002; communal fireworks on 5 November and New Year breakfasts at the Regency Restaurant.

In 2015, the RSAS was a founding member of the Regency Square Regeneration Partnership, which hopes to receive funding, through an agreement between

Brighton & Hove City Council and British Airways i360, to renovate the gardens.

The heritage board in Regency Square's north garden was funded externally but designed by RSAS. It shows an 1820s image of the square donated by Mr Roger Amerena.

The Pierrotters were invited to perform in the square for the Royal Wedding celebrations organised
by the society in 1986
© Suzanne Hinton

A peep into other houses

2 Regency Square

Dr William King lived at No. 2 from 1828 until at least 1830. Dr King was an early advocate and active promoter of the co-operative movement, preceding the Rochdale Pioneers by 15 years. He was one of the main supporters of the Brighton Co-operative Benevolent Fund, launched in 1828. He was also physician at the Brighton Hove and Preston Provident Dispensary, founded in 1837 to provide medicine to the poor.

7 Regency Square

A boarding house since at least the 1830s, No. 7 continued as such until it was named Leander House around 1902 and became a hotel. Here, in 1964, Lady Adonia McIndoe *died from an overdose of sleeping pills after drinking the equivalent of more than six glasses of whiskey*. The verdict was *Misadventure*.

More sinister events were to take place in 2007, when police discovered that serial killer Peter Tobin had lodged at 7 Regency Square in the early 1970s. The Times newspaper reported: (Tobin's) *address was a Georgian townhouse in Regency Square, Brighton … The house is now in one of Brighton's most fashionable squares. Then it was made up of seven seedy bedsits.* The small back patio of the house was dug up. No human remains were found.

In 1975, two years after Tobin left, the house was gutted by a massive fire. It was rebuilt as apartments.

10 Regency Square

For several years during the 1820s, this was the home of the Reverend William Hanson. No relation to Joshua Flesher Hanson, the Rev Hanson was the son of a wealthy Hammersmith iron merchant. He never had the *cure of souls,* meaning that he was never a rector, vicar or even a humble curate. He did, however, officiate at weddings in Brighton and, in 1827, was described as *one of the domestic Chaplains of the Marquess of Downshire and residing in Brighton.* At the time, the Rev Hanson was paying rates on both Nos. 10 and 35 Regency Square.

He disappeared while supposedly on a trip to Ireland in 1827 *to visit celebrated places.* No one heard from him for months. Newspapers published a description in the hope of finding him:

> The Gentleman is about thirty-seven years of age, five feet ten inches high, rather stout, good complexion, oval face, good nose, light brown hair and whiskers, grey eyes, rather short sighted and always an eye glass.
>
> *Saunders News-Letter 4 August 1827*

The description was no doubt supplied by his wife, Eliza, who offered a reward of 100 guineas to anyone finding her husband. And then, in mid-October, this rather sardonic comment appeared in several national newspapers:

> REV. WILLIAM HANSON. This person, who has been advertised at every post-office window in the three kingdoms, and who has been mourned for as dead by his wife and family during some months, has been found "alive and merry" at *Havre de Grace.*
>
> *Syndicated item October 1827*

Had the Rev Hanson had a breakdown? His wife later instructed her solicitor to sue newspapers regarding the *libellous insinuations which have appeared in some daily prints, to state that mental disease was the cause of all that was mysterious.*

Doctors

Several physicians and surgeons set up consulting rooms in Regency Square in the 19th century. Arguably the most famous of these was physician Dr Edward Charles Robson Roose. He settled at 44 Regency Square in 1875 and moved to London a decade later. He was family doctor to the Churchills. In the spring of 1886, young Winston fell ill at his school in Brunswick Road, Hove. At the behest of the young lad's parents, the great doctor returned to Brighton and is credited with helping to save Winston's life.

In 1845, Nos. 17, 18, 19, 23, 24 and 43 were listed as the residences, and most likely consulting rooms, of surgeons. In the 1860s, the square even boasted a homeopathic practitioner, Mr Ackworth at No. 3.

Doctors mainly seemed to cluster around the north-west corner of the square. The father and son, James and Richard Dill, were variously at Nos. 19 and 21; the Allens, Thomas and Marcus, were at Nos. 16 and 20. This corner was perhaps convenient for Richard Moore's chemist shop at 67 Preston Street, abutting 21 Regency Square.

Regency Square in the 1870s. Note the large number of gas lamps surrounding the garden. The elaborate, dark railings and gates in the foreground are those of the West Pier. The square has simpler, white or grey railings.
James Gray Collection, © Philippe Garner, Courtesy of the Regency Society

22 Regency Square

In 1824, the following advertisement appeared in the Brighton Gazette:

> **22, REGENCY SQUARE**
>
> MRS REEVES will be happy to admit into her Establishment, six Young Ladies as daily pupils, whom she would instruct in every branch of Education, with or without the assistance of Masters.

Like several of the other schools established in the early days of the square, this one was doomed to a short existence. Mrs Brightwell, an estate agent, took over the ground floor around 1827 and remained in business there for 30 years.

Mr Jenner's estate agency then occupied the premises, as Jenner and Son in the 1860s, Jenner and Dell in the early 1870s. Mr Loader added his name to the firm in 1909, by which time the business had expanded into 23 Regency Square.

The firm often dealt with prestigious properties. In 1928, they were selling Western House, the home of Viscount Astor, later demolished for the building of Embassy Court.

38 Regency Square

Compared to the majority of the houses in the square, No. 38 is a small property. During the early part of the 20th century, it had been extended across its back garden to incorporate a one-storey mews cottage. When it was bought by a developer in 1972, he found that the house was divided into 15 separate areas of accommodation, housing some 18–20 people:

- A manager occupied the two large rooms in the basement. There was an outhouse with a toilet and an arched brick construction that appeared to be a bomb shelter.

- Each of the two main ground floor rooms (originally the dining room and a parlour) contained a bed, a one-ring gas hob, a wash-hand basin and a cupboard. These rooms were let out weekly as holiday accommodation. Typically, one family would occupy each room.

- At the rear of the ground floor were two rooms: a bed-sitting room with a window overlooking a dark courtyard and a windowless kitchen. This was the home of a couple in their late 70s.

- The three units on the ground floor shared a toilet.

- The grand balcony room had been divided into two, each equipped in the same way as the rooms on the ground floor. The smaller of the two rooms measured approximately 6ft x 8ft and was home to a single man.

- A shared bathroom and toilet had been installed in what had been the corridor.

This pattern continued up the house and into the two attic rooms.

39 Regency Square

During the Great Storm of October 1987, a chimney crashed down though the roof of the house, pinning a sleeping student in his bed for several hours. Fortunately the student survived, but spent many months in hospital. The house suffered major damage and was uninhabitable until January 1989. Almost exactly 12 years later to the day, the event was portrayed in an episode of the television series *999*. Several of the firemen who had risked their lives rescuing the student re-enacted the parts they had played in 1987.

More than 100 years previously, the property had caused a lesser upset, but one which has entered legal text books. In January 1851, Mr Stephen Prescott White bought 39 Regency Square at an auction sale. When he finally went to view his purchase for the first time, he was horrified to find that the house had no view of the sea. He sued the vendor, claiming misrepresentation. The judge would have none of it. *You should have looked before you bought* would be a fair summary of the judgement. Law students have to learn the case of White v. Bradshaw to this day.

REGENCY SQUARE

Eligible and valuable Freehold Property, Brighton, Sussex

TO BE SOLD BY AUCTION

By Mr. F. SHOTTER

One Monday, June 16th, 1823, at Seven o'clock in The evening, at the Old Ship Tavern, in 2 Lots

Two elegant and substantially-built FREEHOLD HOUSES, situate and being Nos. 39 and 40, the East side in Regency Square; comprising on the Basement – A housekeeper's-room, a good kitchen, with convenient offices, vaults, &c. First Floor – Two excellent parlours with folding doors, water closet, &c. Second Floor – An elegant drawing room, with veranda in front, commanding views of the sea and the lawn, an excellent bed room behind. Third Floor – Two good bed-rooms with three attics over.

Further particulars may be known of Mr. F. SHOTTER, Auctioneer, Appraiser, Estate, House, and Commercial Agent, adjoining the Theatre, New Road, Brighton.

Sussex Advertiser, 9 June 1823.

Nos. 39 and 40 are, in fact, on the north side of the square, to the east of the central palace front and have no sea view.

40 Regency Square

In the 1880s, a Mrs Green ran a boarding house at No. 40. In the 1980s another Mrs Green moved into the property. Before her marriage she was Christine Bygraves, daughter of popular performer Max Bygraves. It was not unusual to see Mr Bygraves' white Rolls Royce parked outside the house. Mrs Green's own claim to fame was as the first Body Shop franchise holder. The Body Shop had opened in Kensington Gardens in 1976 and by 1979 Mrs Green had opened the first franchise shop in George Street, Hove.

42–44 Regency Square

William Silverthorne came from Frome in Somerset in about 1830 to run a livery stable in Upper Regency Mews. He and his family lived in various houses adjacent to the mews, including 42, 43 and 44 Regency Square, and 37 Russell Square.

> **To BE SOLD**, a great bargain at Silverthorne's Regency Mews, Regency Square, Brighton, a very **HANDSOME CHARIOT**, nearly new (having had only about four months use) painted yellow, the lining and reclining squabs drab, coach-box, boot and dash leather in front, swinging footboard and standards behind, the whole complete and warranted. Parted with for no fault but the owner having given up his establishment. - NB. Horses let on the job at the above Mews.
>
> *Brighton Gazette 2 October 1834*

One of William's sons, Isaac, joined the business. His other son, James, went on to grander things. James was often known as Colonel Silverthorne as he was a volunteer in the 1st Administrative Brigade of the Sussex Artillery Volunteers. Later, he became an Alderman of Brighton.

46a Regency Square

46a was the premises of Edmund Scott's architectural practice between 1864 and 1895. Scott designed St Bartholomew's, the tallest church in Brighton, and St Saviour's in Ditchling Road, as well as the remodelling and expansion of several other Brighton churches. He also designed the Royal Sussex Regiment drill hall in Church Street. This building is now an antiques warehouse.

In the early part of the 20th century, No. 46a was variously a printers and milliners. It was a café in the 1930s, a tailor's premises in the 1940s and 1950s, a dentist's surgery in the 1970s.

48 Regency Square

Thomas and Martha Tanner lived at No. 48 from the 1830s until the mid-1850s. Thomas was a plumber, a man who worked with lead. In 1852, while checking the lead on a house in Trafalgar Street, he fell from the roof to the basement, injuring his back so seriously that at first it was assumed to be broken. The Tanners had already been supplementing their income by letting rooms. Now that Thomas' working days were over, the family relied on running No. 48 as a lodging house.

Between 1888 and 1893, No. 48 was the family home of Captain William Poland, the master of the West Pier.

50 Regency Square

The early history of No. 50 had been long forgotten until, in the late 1970s, a family moved in and started renovation work. When the plaster was removed in the basement, a 19th century commercial bread oven was found extending under the pavement of Regency Square. A massive coal storage area was found running under Queensbury Mews.

No. 50 had been a bakery for almost four decades, from at least 1839. The baker was Mr John Hollingham, then Mrs Elizabeth Hollingham. In the late 1870s No. 50 was a greengrocer's shop, later a laundry. In the early part of the 20th century, it was a lodging house. Until the end of the 20th century, the words St Margaret's Guest House could be faintly seen high on its west wall.

The Stratheden Hotel, 59–63 Regency Square

In 1895, 80 per cent of the houses in Regency Square were either boarding houses or lodging houses. It was then that Nos. 61 and 62 were first called The Stratheden. Later, as The Stratheden Mansions Hotel, it occupied five houses and was one of the largest and longest surviving hotels in the square.

During WW2 the Stratheden Mansions Hotel was a training centre for pilots. One of the pilots billeted there was 20-year-old Roman Skulski of the Polish Air Force (PAF). After surviving appalling conditions in Poland, Roman managed to escape to France, finally reaching Britain in 1942. He attended the PAF/RAF training course held in Abbotts Hotel (67–69 Regency Square), taking his meals in the Metropole Hotel.

Roman recalled that *at the centre of the square there was an underground shelter that we used every time German planes arrived, and sometimes for "smooching".* One of the girls he may have been "smooching" might well have been Joan Malik's sister, Edna. Joan recounts in her book, *The Many Faces of Love,* how she and a friend would spend hours sitting in Regency Square *listening to an accordion being played in the Polish quarters.* Edna married Roman Skulski on 21 June 1946.

67 Regency Square

According to Melville's directory, Sir Charles Barry was the occupant of No. 67 in 1858. As well as the Houses of Parliament, Sir Charles designed Brighton's St Peter's Church and Royal Sussex County Hospital, St Andrew's Church in Hove and the Queen's Park Pepper Pot.

Regency Square lawns 1945.
Courtesy of Historic England

What Hanson did next

Regency Square was Joshua Flesher Hanson's first venture into property development. In 1823, with two thirds of the square either under construction or complete, he was sufficiently confident of its success to take part in the Notting Hill Square (now Campden Hill Square) and Ladbroke Estate developments in London. In the 1830s he began work on other London developments, at Hyde Park Gate and Kensington Gore.

There is no evidence that Joshua Flesher Hanson ever built a house for himself in Brighton, but it's possible that he considered doing so. In 1820, he bought a plot of land at the bottom of what is now Hampton Place and Spring Street. We don't know what he subsequently did with that plot. He did, however, build grand houses for himself in Notting Hill Square and Kensington Gore.

Joshua and Nancy Hanson had seven children, two of whom died in infancy. Two of their sons, Stephen and Alfred, rose to the professional classes by becoming, respectively, a clergyman and a lawyer. Another son, Cyrus, continued running the Henllys brickworks after Joshua's death.

Joshua died suddenly during a brief business visit to Jersey in April 1847. He is buried at Kensal Green cemetery in north Kensington. His death was announced in the London Evening Standard, the Monmouthshire Merlin and the Oxford Journal. The Monmouthshire newspaper referred to him as *a coal owner of Newport*. The London and Oxford papers described him as *Mr Joshua Flesher Hanson of Hyde Park Gate, Kensington Gore*. The Oxford Journal included the detail that he had died *of apoplexy*, which implies a heart attack or stroke. He had drawn up his will only weeks before.

Portrait of Joshua Flesher Hanson by Michael Blackmore for the Henllys tramroad information board. Main image supplied by Phil Jenkins of Industrial Gwent and reproduced with kind permission of the Blackmore family.

Joshua Flesher Hanson

He bequeathed all of his property, including some Regency Square freeholds still in his possession, to his five surviving children.[23] His will stipulates an annuity of £200 a year (roughly £16,000 in today's money) for his widow, to be funded by the income from properties. His widow survived him by only one year, but there were extensive mortgages outstanding on the Hyde Park Gate development. Partly in order to meet these commitments, Hanson's heirs began to sell off elements of his property portfolio. Over the next 11 years, they gradually disposed of assets, including the remaining Regency Square freeholds.

---

23 Joshua Flesher Hanson's will, written in January 1847, names his nephew John Austin (Junior) as trustee. Austin was to arrange an annuity for the widow and manage the rest of the estate on behalf of Hanson's three sons and unmarried daughter, Theodosia. Hanson's married daughter, Mary, was to receive only £20 *for mourning*, because she was *sufficiently provided for already*. Six weeks later, and just three weeks before he died, Hanson changed his will. His widow would still receive her annuity, but all five sons and daughters were to share the rest of his estate. Someone – possibly her lawyer husband – had insisted on Mary receiving a share.

Freehold Estates And Ground Rent

REGENCY COLONNADE, REGENCY SQUARE, BRIGHTON

Mr Wilkinson has received instructions from the Devises in Trust, under the Will of the late Joshua Flesher Hanson, Esquire, to Sell by Public Auction, at his Estate Sale Rooms, North Street, Brighton, on Thursday, the 14th day of June, 1855, at Two for Three o'clock precisely,

THE FOLLOWING IMPORTANT PROPERTY:-

In Lots

No. 1, REGENCY COLONNADE, REGENCY SQUARE, a substantially-built House and Premises known as "Regency Tavern", containing a spacious Bar, good Bar Parlour and Public Room, two excellent Rooms on the floor above, three Bed Rooms, good Kitchen, Wash-house, Yard, Cellarage, and Outbuilding, let to Mr Henry Gaston, on an agreement for a lease for 7, 14, or 21 years, from June, 1853, at the low rent of £34 per annum.

Also, A WELL-BUILT HOUSE WITH SHOP, situate and being No. 2, REGENCY COLONNADE, containing good Shop and Parlour, Five Rooms above, Two Rooms on Basement, with Yard, Outbuildings, Water Closet and Wash-house in the rear, in the occupation of Mr John Wood, on a yearly tenancy, at the very inadequate rent of £30 per annum.

Also, No. 3, REGENCY COLONNADE, with similar accommodation and Corner SHOP, in the occupation of Mr William Streeter, as yearly tenant at £35 per annum.

Also REGENCY COTTAGE, REGENCY SQUARE, known as "Regency Dairy", having just been re-built in a substantial and ornamental manner, by Messrs. Field, from the design of a London Architect, with good Shop, Sitting-Room, Two Bed Rooms, Kitchen, Dairy, Wash-house, &c., let to Mr. Edward Jordan, on lease, for 7, 14 or 21 years, from June 1854, at £25 9*s* per annum.

Also, EXTENSIVE COACH HOUSE AND STABLING for nine horses situate in REGENCY MEWS, immediately contiguous to premises in Preston Street. The Stabling is all brick-built, and is in three divisions, each division having a court entrance enclosed by gates. This property is held on Lease by Mr. Henry Kennard for 21 years from September, 1849, at a net rent of £100 per annum.

Full descriptive particulars, with conditions of sale, may be had 10 days prior to the Sale of Messrs. Church and Son, Solicitors, 9, Bedford Row, London; and of the Auctioneer, at his Estate and Sale Rooms, North Street, Brighton.

Brighton Gazette, 31 May 1855.

The address of the Regency Tavern as No. 1 Regency Colonnade is incorrect. The Regency Tavern was No. 3, the corner shop was No. 1

Hanson family tree

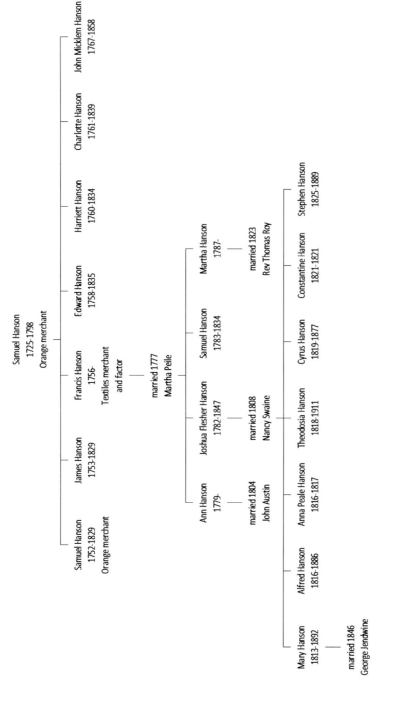

Samuel Hanson
1725-1798
Orange merchant

Samuel Hanson
1752-1829
Orange merchant

James Hanson
1753-1829

Francis Hanson
1756-
Textiles merchant
and factor

married 1777
Martha Peile

Edward Hanson
1758-1835

Harriett Hanson
1760-1834

Charlotte Hanson
1761-1839

John Micklem Hanson
1767-1858

Ann Hanson
1779-

married 1804
John Austin

Joshua Flesher Hanson
1782-1847

married 1808
Nancy Swaine

Samuel Hanson
1783-1834

Martha Hanson
1787-

married 1823
Rev Thomas Roy

Mary Hanson
1813-1892

married 1846
George Jendwine

Alfred Hanson
1816-1886

Anna Peale Hanson
1816-1817

Theodosia Hanson
1818-1911

Cyrus Hanson
1819-1877

Constantine Hanson
1821-1821

Stephen Hanson
1825-1889

In addition to the seven children shown in the family tree, Samuel Hanson had six others who died in infancy.

Regency-square
Sunday 8 September 1822

My dear Sister,
I have seen him! I have seen the King! It was Monday last. I was just helping the Mistress dress her hair before she went down to dinner. We saw lights shining and a crowd around the corner house. A carriage drew up and we could see it quite clearly as there were flambeaus on the house and the carriage. And then the King got out and went into the house. The Mistress says the house belongs to Sir Richard Borough – but he and his family must be like the Master and the Mistress. We do not often see them here in Brighton. The Mistress says they have a grand house in Portland-place in London which she has visited and a place in the county. Just imagine – all those houses. How I would love to work in a place in the country. Can you keep a secret my dear? I may never have to work again. I'm walking out with John, the postman. He comes to the house regularly, and my job is to speak to him. I always know it's him as postmen are allowed to knock only twice – the Master's guests knock several times and that's Mary's job to answer the door when they come. He hands over the letters and I have to go to the Master or the Mistress to get the money to pay for the letter. He always stops to chat with me. Don't tell mother just yet but I have high hopes …
Your loving sister
Polly

Sources

History of Brighton

A History of the County of Sussex: Volume 7, ed. L. F. Salzman, 1940

An Historical Atlas of Sussex, ed. Leslie and Short, 1999

A Peep into the Past: Brighton in the Olden Time, J. G. Bishop, 1892

Baxter's Brighton Directory, 1822

Encyclopaedia of Brighton, Timothy Carder, 1990

Georgian Brighton, Sue Berry, 1980 and 2005

History of Brighthelmston, J. Erredge, 1862

Life in Brighton, Clifford Musgrave, 1981

The Brighton Garrison 1793–1900, R. C. Grant

The Windmills and Millers of Brighton, H. T. Dawes, Sussex Archaeological Society

The Hansons

Ancestry.co.uk

Blackwell Hall Factors, 1795–1799, Conrad Gill, The Economic History Review, Vol. 6, 1954

Brighton rate book 1802

Brighton street directories 1799–1800

British Newspaper Archive

Hansons of Eastcheap, Maurice Harp, The Perfin Society Bulletin, December 1996

Industrial Gwent www.industrialgwent.co.uk

London and Westminster directories and rate books, 1782 and 1794

London Metropolitan Archives

Records of London's Livery Companies

Romantic Poetry by Women: a Bibliography, 1770–1835, J. R. de J. Jackson

South Wales Coalfield www.agor.org.uk/cwm/themes/Life/society/coal_owners

Survey of London, Volumes 37 and 38, North Kensington and South Kensington Museums Area, ed. F. H. W. Sheppard, 1973 and 1975

The Brickworks of Torfaen, Lawrence Skuse

The National Archives

www.welshcoalmines.co.uk

Building Regency Square

Original documents at The Keep, including Brighton rate books (1826 and 1834), and contracts relating to Regency Square land and houses (references below), with supporting information from:

Country Life

London Gardens Trust

RIBA

The Condition of the Working-Class in England 1209–2004, Gregory Clark, (including dataset published by the International Institute of Social History)

The Customary Acre: An indeterminate Measure, Robert S. Dilley. The Agricultural History Review Vol. 23, 1975

The French Wars and the Industrial Revolution, Patrick O'Brien, published in Refresh, Spring 1992

The Regency Town House

Traditional Building Materials, Matthew Slocombe, Shire Library, 2012

Treatise on the Progressive Improvement and Present State of the Manufactures in Metal, Vol 2, Iron and Steel, John Holland, 1833

University of Nottingham's Department of Manuscripts and Special Collections.

www.pubshistory.com

References for original documents held at The Keep

Belle Vue House and the site of Regency Square:

AMS 6454/55; BH/G/2/1579; BH/P/ES/AX/60; SAS/BRI/18; SAS/B/79; SAS/B/80

Building the square:

ACC 11871/4/1; ACC 4194/1; ACC 469/14; ACC 5369/23; ACC 8553/2; ACC 8767/1; AMS 6717/1; AMS 6717/3/1; BH/G/2/1759; BH/P/ES/AX/41; BH/P/ES/AX/60; HOW 13/6; HOW 7/6; HOW 21/10

Building alteration plans:

DB/D 8/2527; DB/D 8/3384; DB/D 8/2449; DB/D/8/1585;
DB/D/139/80/1/377; DB/D/142/1872/11; DB/D/142/1875/59;
DB/D/142/1877/5; DB/D/142/1888/117; DB/D/142/1894/361;
DB/D/142/1896/313; DB/D/142/1899/33; DB/D/142/1905/280;

Bills and tender documents for town commissioners' contractors:

DB/B/60/63/1/12; DB/B/71/150

Minutes of town commissioners' meetings 1826–1832:

DB/B/60/60/1/1–5

The Life and Times of Regency Square

Ancestry.co.uk

Archive of the Regency Square Area Society

Brighton & Hove City Council

Brighton street directories 1822–1973 (various sources)

British Newspaper Archives

Encyclopaedia of Brighton, Timothy Carder, 1990

Minutes of Regency Square Management Committee

The Regency Society of Brighton and Hove

Notes

Polly is a fictional character, but the events and details in her letters are drawn from fact.

Estimates of the present day value of pre-decimal prices are based on the National Archives currency converter.

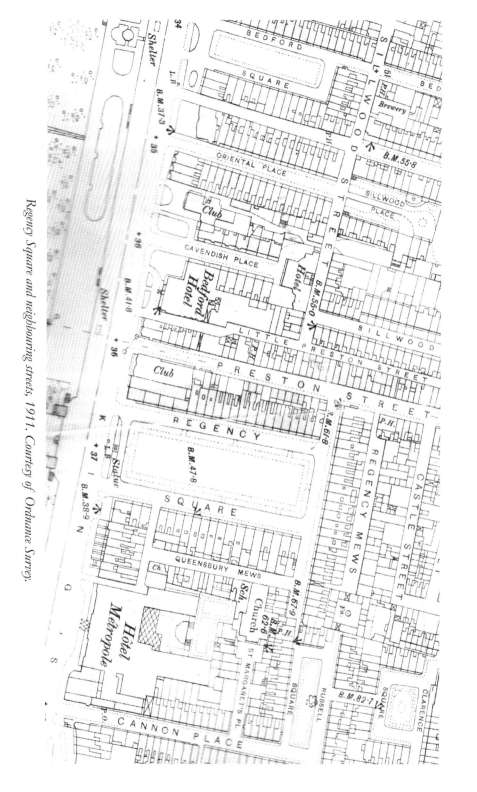

Regency Square and neighbouring streets, 1911. Courtesy of Ordnance Survey.

Subscribers

The idea for this book came from the Regency Square Area Society who have paid for the printing and publishing costs, supported by advance subscriptions from the following people. All proceeds from sales of the book will go to the Regency Square Area Society.

Ros Boulden
Nicola, David and Bandit Floyd
Ken and Marion McClymont
Kit Carson
Dorothy Everitt
Janina Liu
R. and B. Healey
Geoffrey Barton
Diana Dunn
Shoshana and Brian Foster
Wendy Forrester
Paula Brookes
Mary Hunter
Julie Wright
Mike Davies
Suzanne and Roger Hinton
Richard Allsop
Michael Napier
Nigel Rose
Corinne Turnbull
Jennie Hinton and Rob Baillie
Trix Webber
Tony Evans
Sandra Strand
Alan Hinton & Deborah Newbold
Mark Bednall
Kevin Wilsher
Barry Wilsher
Sarah Anne Winterbottom
Diane Page
Emilio Savvides

Index

Abbott James Vercoe.............................52–53

Actresses Franchise League.........*See* Moore Decima

Attree Thomas.................................27, 45, 47

Austin John 16, 19, 20

Austin John (Junior)................................120

Awsiter Dr John 6

BA i360 ....81, 94, 109

Backwell (Somerset)...................................18

Barry Sir Charles (architect).....................118

Bedford Square............................9, 20, 39, 91

Belle Vue Field. 15

Belle Vue House...12–16, 19–22, 26, 39–40, 48, 50–51

Birch Eugenius (engineer) 94

Blackwell Hall 11

Body Shop.................*See* Bygraves Christine

Boer War (South African campaign) ...92–93

Brighthelmston....................2-5, 9, 10, 13, 15

Brighton Corporation Act 1831..............107

Brighton Improvement Act 1884 ......78, 103

Brighton Revisited (film) 60

Brighton Rock (film) 57

Brunswick Square..................................39, 92

bungaroosh (building material) 29

Burton Decimus (architect) 39

Bygraves Max and Christine.....................115

Chain Pier..73

China Doll Restaurant 51

Churchill Winston...............................99, 112

City of London 11, 12, 16, 23, 75

Clarke Cecil Somers 92

Clarke Somers...........................92, 94, 101–3

Cliff Butts 3, 4, 12, 13, 22

Coutts Mrs............ *See* St Albans Duchess of

Coutts Sir Thomas 48

covenants..........26, 31, 40, 66, 67, 78, 101–2

Denman and Son (architects)....................80

Esmond Eva (née Moore) 97, 99

Esmond Jill...99

fairs 15

falconry...50

Feld Alf (former Mayor of Brighton).........83

French Protestant Church 87

garages 84–85, 86, 88

George IV Hotel 108

Hanson Cyrus 16, 18, 119

Hanson family....................11, 119, 120, 122

Hanson Francis....11–16, 19, 20, 22, 23, 122

Hanson Joshua Flesher 11–12, 16–19, 22, 23, 64–68, 101, 119, 120, 122

Hanson Martha (poet)........................12, 122

Hanson Rev. William 111

Hanson Samuel....................................11, 122

Hartwell Charles (sculptor).......................93

Henllys colliery and brickworks..16–18, 119

Hollingham Elizabeth (baker) 117

Jenner and Dell (estate agents) 104, 106, 113

Jordan Edward (dairyman) 58, 121

Kemp Thomas.. 4

Kemp Thomas Read......................19, 22, 65

Kennedy Nigel (violinist)......*See* Stoner family

King Dr William.......................................110

Kings Road 13, 14, 22, 27, 44, 47–48, 52, 83, 85–87, 91

Lawson and Sons (jewellers).......................51

Little Preston Street.................13, 22, 50, 89

Little Tower Street Academy................16, 18

Llantarnam ....*See* Henllys

Lower Regency Mews.*See* Queensbury Mews

Mackie William (surveyor) 28, 44–46

Mellon Harriot..... *See* St Albans Duchess of

Melrose Restaurant 13

Metropole Hotel...118

military encampments 7

Moore Decima.................... *See* Moore family

Moore family................................95–99, 112

Napoleonic wars..20

Newport (Wales) 16, 18, 119

Norfolk Hotel................................. 73, 83, 91

Olivier Laurence.................... *See* Esmond Jill

Pertwee family 99–100

Pink String and Sealing Wax (play) 95, 100

Pocock Shadrach (builder) 26–28

Poland Captain .... *See* West Pier

Polly letters .... viii, 32, 68, 125, 128

Portland House Hotel 108

Preston Street.. 13, 20, 28, 29, 65, 77, 82, 84, 91, 95–97, 112, 121

privileged houses 78

Queensbury Arms...87

Queensbury Mews 34, 41, 47, 66, 77, 85–88, 106, 117

railings 21, 27, 30, 78, 101, 104, 107, 112

Regency Colonnade 61–63, 64, 121

Regency Cottage..58

Regency Mews.. 6, 19, 29, 56, 84–85, 97, 116

Regency Restaurant 44, 51, 108

Regency Society.......................................80–81

Regency Square Area Society 108, 129

Regency Tavern 58, 61, 63, 121

Regents Place 66

Restall John (surveyor) 20, 23, 39

Robison James 26, 40, 91, 92, 101

Rooky's Club..51

Royal Sovereign (Preston Street)...............82

Russell Dr Richard 5–6, 20

Russell Mews.......................................85, 108

Russell Square . 20, 36, 47, 55, 57, 61, 63, 84, 116

Scott Edmund (architect) 116

Silverthorne family............. 84, 101, 104, 116

St Albans Duchess of 48–51

St Margaret's Church 54, 58–59, 86, 87

St Margaret's Schools................................106

St Nicholas' Church 12, 44

stables..... 13, 19, 50, 66, 84, 85, 88, 106, 116

Stoner family...82

storms 2-3, 94, 114

Stratheden Mansions Hotel 117

Street Mrs Sarah 20–22, 25, 39

Streeter John 14, 121

Swaine family.......................................23, 66

tennis 106, 107

The Hole in the Wall. *See* Queensbury Arms

Tony's Café 51

twitten 55, 57, 58, 61, 63, 89

Upper Regency Mews...... *See* Regency Mews

Vallance John 65

Waterloo Square 24

West Laine 3–5, 7, 12, 16, 19, 65

West Mill.......................................3, 14–15, 22

West Pier........................... 7, 56, 94, 112, 117

Western Road...5

wharf 13–14, 19, 22, 29

Wigney George...27

Wigney Isaac Newton...........................27, 66

Wilds Amon and Amon Henry............42–47

Wilds Amon Henry......................................47

Wilds and Busby...39

WW1 .... 104, 105

WW2 ....51, 78, 85, 104, 107, 117